T0181191

IFIP Advances in Information and Communication Technology

465

IFIP – The International Federation for Information Processing

IFIP was founded in 1960 under the auspices of UNESCO, following the First World Computer Congress held in Paris the previous year. An umbrella organization for societies working in information processing, IFIP's aim is two-fold: to support information processing within its member countries and to encourage technology transfer to developing nations. As its mission statement clearly states,

IFIP's mission is to be the leading, truly international, apolitical organization which encourages and assists in the development, exploitation and application of information technology for the benefit of all people.

IFIP is a non-profitmaking organization, run almost solely by 2500 volunteers. It operates through a number of technical committees, which organize events and publications. IFIP's events range from an international congress to local seminars, but the most important are:

- The IFIP World Computer Congress, held every second year;
- Open conferences;
- Working conferences.

The flagship event is the IFIP World Computer Congress, at which both invited and contributed papers are presented. Contributed papers are rigorously refereed and the rejection rate is high.

As with the Congress, participation in the open conferences is open to all and papers may be invited or submitted. Again, submitted papers are stringently refereed.

The working conferences are structured differently. They are usually run by a working group and attendance is small and by invitation only. Their purpose is to create an atmosphere conducive to innovation and development. Refereeing is also rigorous and papers are subjected to extensive group discussion.

Publications arising from IFIP events vary. The papers presented at the IFIP World Computer Congress and at open conferences are published as conference proceedings, while the results of the working conferences are often published as collections of selected and edited papers.

Any national society whose primary activity is about information processing may apply to become a full member of IFIP, although full membership is restricted to one society per country. Full members are entitled to vote at the annual General Assembly, National societies preferring a less committed involvement may apply for associate or corresponding membership. Associate members enjoy the same benefits as full members, but without voting rights. Corresponding members are not represented in IFIP bodies. Affiliated membership is open to non-national societies, and individual and honorary membership schemes are also offered.

More information about this series at http://www.springer.com/series/6102

Tharam Dillon (Ed.)

Artificial Intelligence in Theory and Practice IV

4th IFIP TC 12 International Conference
on Artificial Intelligence, IFIP AI 2015
Held as Part of WCC 2015
Daejeon, South Korea, October 4–7, 2015
Proceedings

 Springer

Editor
Tharam Dillon
La Trobe University
Melbourne
Australia

ISSN 1868-4238   ISSN 1868-422X (electronic)
IFIP Advances in Information and Communication Technology
ISBN 978-3-319-38732-1   ISBN 978-3-319-25261-2 (eBook)
DOI 10.1007/978-3-319-25261-2

Springer Cham Heidelberg New York Dordrecht London

Printed on acid-free paper

Springer International Publishing AG Switzerland is part of Springer Science+Business Media
(www.springer.com)

Preface

The papers in this volume comprise the refereed proceedings of the conference Artificial Intelligence in Theory and Practice (IFIP AITP 2015), which formed part of the 23rd World Computer Congress of IFIP, the International Federation for Information Processing (WCC-2015), held in Daejeon, Korea, in October 2015.

The conference was organized by the IFIP Technical Committee on Artificial Intelligence (Technical Committee 12) and its Working Groups. TC12 was formed in 1989. It now has members representing 33 national computer societies, together with representatives of the ACM and the IEEE, and has nine working groups covering major topics in artificial intelligence (AI). The aims of TC12 are:

- To foster the development and understanding of AI and its applications worldwide.
- To promote interdisciplinary exchanges between AI and other fields of information processing.
- To contribute to the overall aims and objectives and further development of IFIP as the international body for information processing.

TC12 carries out these activities through its nine working groups that are as follows:
WG 12.1 - Knowledge Representation and Reasoning led by Dr. Matthias Thimm
WG 12.2 - Machine Learning and Data Mining led by Prof. Zhongzhi Shi
WG 12.3 - Intelligent Agents led by Prof. Helder Coelho
WG 12.4 - Web Semantics led by Prof. Elizabeth Chang
WG 12.5 - Artificial Intelligence Applications led by Prof. Ilias Maglogiannis
WG 12.6 - Knowledge Management led by Prof. Eunika Mercier-Laurent
WG 12.7 - Social Networking Semantics and Collective Intelligence led by Dr. Pieter De Leenheer
WG 12.8 - Intelligent Bioinformatics and Biomedical Systems led by Prof. Phoebe Chen
WG 12.9 - Computational Intelligence led by Prof. Tharam Dillon

For AITP 2015, we received submissions from authors that highlighted the benefits of AI technology for industry and services. We also received papers that highlighted the benefits of using AI in interdisciplinary areas such as bioinformatics. All papers were reviewed by three members and in a very few cases by at least two members of our Program Committee and final decisions were made by the program chair. The best papers were selected for the conference as long papers and are included in this volume. The international nature of IFIP is amply reflected in the large number of countries represented here.

I thank the Program Committee members, for all their efforts and for reviewing papers under a very tight deadline and maintaining the high quality of the conference. This is the latest in a series of conferences organized by IFIP Technical Committee 12 dedicated to the techniques of artificial intelligence and their real-world applications. The wide range and importance of these applications is clearly indicated by the papers in this volume. Further information about TC12 can be found on our website at http://www.ifiptc12.org.

August 2015   Tharam Dillon

Organization

Conference and Program Chair

Tharam Dillon   La Trobe University, Australia

Publications Chair

Omar Hussain   UNSW Canberra, Australia

Web Master

Naeem Janjua   UNSW Canberra, Australia

Program Committee Members

Tharam Dillon	La Trobe University, Australia
Ilias Maglogiannis	University of Piraeus, Greece
Elize Ehlers	University of Johanesburg, South Africa
Zhongzhi Shi	Chinese Academy of Sciences, China
Roman Slowinski	Poznan University of Technology, Poland
Eunika Mercier-Laurent	Knowledge and Innovation Management and IAE Lyon University, France
Matthias Thimm	Universität Koblenz, Germany
Nenad Stefanovic	University of Kragujevac, Serbia
Serena Villata	Inria Sophia Antipolis, France
Peter Haddawy	Asian Institute of Technology, Thailand
Oliver Obst	CSIRO ICT Centre, Australia
Farookh Khadeer Hussain	University of Technology, Australia
Omar Khadeer Hussain	University of New South Wales, Australia
Naeem Khalid Janjua	University of New South Wales, Australia
Geoffrey Holmes	University of Waikato, New Zealand
James Harland	RMIT University, Australia
Merlin Teodosia Suarez	De La Salle University, Philippines
Guandong Xu	University of Technology, Sydney, Australia
Chengqi Zhang	University of Technology, Sydney, Australia
Fukuta Naoki	Shizuoka University, Japan
Tru Cao	Ho Chi Minh City University of Technology, Vietnam
Aizawa Akiko	National Institute of Informatics, Japan
Jiamou Liu	Auckland University of Technology, New Zealand
Reinhard Moratz	University of Maine, USA
Vasile Palade	Coventry University, UK

Contents

Intelligent Decision Support Systems

Artificial Intelligence Techniques
in Bio Medicine

Efficacy of the *Fuzzy Polynucleotide Space* in Phylogenetic Tree Construction

Awanti Sambarey[1($\boxtimes$)] and Ashok Deshpande[2,3]

[1] Molecular Biophysics Unit, Indian Institute of Science, Bangalore, India
awanti@mbu.iisc.ernet.in
[2] Berkeley Initiative in Soft Computing(BISC)-Special Interest Group- (SIG)-Environment Management Systems (EMS), University of California at Berkeley, Berkeley, USA
ashok_deshpande@hotmail.com
[3] College of Engineering Pune, Pune, India

Abstract. The study of evolutionary relationships is an important endeavor in the field of Bioinformatics. The fuzzification of genomes led to the introduction of a "*fuzzy polynucleotide space*", which has been successfully used in classification and clustering of amino acids, thereby suggesting a possible application in phylogeny. As phylogenetic trees illustrate similarities and evolutionary relationships among different taxa, through this study we attempt to determine the efficacy of the fuzzy polynucleotide space in phylogenetic tree reconstruction, and discuss its implications in evolutionary biology.

Keywords: Fuzzy polynucleotide space · NTV metric · Phylogenetic tree construction

1 Introduction

Sequence analysis and comparative genomics play a central role in Bioinformatics. Phylogenetic relationships among organisms are established on the basis of molecular sequences, in order to understand their course of evolution and ancestry. Molecular phylogeny involves building of a relationship tree that shows the probable evolution of various organisms. The conventional tree building approaches are broadly divided into: a) **Distance based approaches**- which take into account the evolutionary distances between all taxa, where the distance represents the number of nucleotide or amino acid changes between sequences. These include methods such as Neighbour Joining, Unweighted Pair Group Mean Average (UPGMA), Minimum Evolution, and alike. b) **Character based approaches**- these include methods such as Maximum Parsimony, Maximum likelihood and Bayesian sequence analysis.

Statistical techniques have played, and will continue to play a pivotal role in sequence analysis. The past decade has witnessed several applications of fuzzy sets and fuzzy logic in bioinformatics, with its successful use in sequence alignment, DNA sequencing, clustering and classification [1,2,3,4]. Fuzzy set theory was first rendered directly accessible to sequence comparisons in the works of Sadegh-Zadeh. He introduced the concept of *Fuzzy Polynucleotides* [5], by transforming nucleic acid

T. Dillon (Ed.): IFIP AI 2015, IFIP AICT 465, pp. 3–16, 2015.
DOI: 10.1007/978-3-319-25261-2_1

sequences into ordered fuzzy sets. The author showed that the genetic code can be considered as a 12 –dimensional code, with each triplet codon XYZ having a 3×4 =12 dimensional fuzzy code, and thus falling as a point in what the author termed as the 12- dimensional *fuzzy polynucleotide space* I=$[0,1]^{12}$, where I $\in$ R.

Torres and Nieto [6] redefined the Fuzzy Polynucleotide Space, based on the fuzzy hypercube concept proposed by Bart Kosko [7]. Taking into account the frequencies of the nucleotides at the three base sites of a codon in the coding sequence, the authors mapped a given polynucleotide on an I^{12} space which they termed as *Fuzzy Polynucleotide Space (FPNS)*. A sequence of any length could thus be mapped on a 12- dimensional vector, facilitating comparison between sequences of varying lengths. A distance metric *d* that determined distances between the fuzzy vectors of any two polynucleotides, was proposed.

Given the fuzzy polynucleotide space for two sequences p and q, where p = (p1, p2, .. pn), q = (q1, q2, . . . , qn) $\in$ In, n=12, the difference between p and q was calculated as:

$$d(p,q) = \frac{\sum_{i=1}^{12} |p_i - q_i|}{\sum_{i=1}^{12} \max \{p_i, q_i\}} \tag{1}$$

The distance metric as defined in Equation (1) is termed as the NTV metric. The authors computed the fuzzy polynucleotide space for two genomes of E. coli and M. tuberculosis, considering only the coding regions of these genomes, and the distance between them was calculated. The approach was further extended and distances between other genomes were computed [8].

The NTV metric has also been used for the classification of amino acids via fuzzy equivalence relation [9]. In their research study, the authors used two different distance functions viz. the Minkowski distance function and the NTV metric. The clusters obtained using the NTV metric were the same as that obtained using the Minkowski distance metric for high values of the similarity degree. Nieto and Torres [10] have suggested the possible use of NTV metric in phylogenetic analysis. With this backdrop, we have, in this sequel, made an attempt to study the efficacy of the NTV metric in phylogenetic reconstruction.

2   Methods

The structured approach is divided into three parts. Section 2.1 deals with data collection, while section 2.2 describes the salient features of sequence analysis, and the results and discussion on phylogenetic tree analysis are presented in section 2.3:

2.1   Data Collection

A total of nine datasets were considered for the detailed study. However, the discussion on the results of three major datasets was considered sufficient to test the hypothesis and draw meaningful conclusions. The other datasets are available on request.

Dataset 1 comprises of polyprotein-coding regions of Dengue type 3 viruses. The viral isolates were chosen from different regions of the world. Dataset 2 represents gyrase B gene sequences from members of the genus Microbacterium. Dataset 3 includes vertebrate mitochondrial cytochrome b sequences. The cyt b genes were taken from representative members of the six classes viz. Mammalia, Reptilia, Amphibia, Aves, Chondrichthyes and Osteichthyes of Sub-Phylum Vertebrata. The other datasets, considered in the detailed analysis include gyrase B gene sequences from Burkholderia, ompA gene sequences from the genus Rickettsia, chloroplast matK gene sequences from the family Tillandsioideae, VLTF-1 genes from Penguin-pox virus, low-molecular weight glutenin subunit genes from tall wheatgrass, and mitochondrial genes from the hawkmoth genus Hyles.

Only protein-coding genes were considered, and the coding sequences were extracted from National Centre for Biotechnology information (NCBI). All the datasets comprised of experimentally validated, non-redundant sequences. For majority of the datasets, the phylogenetic relationships have been well established. Generic and species information were obtained from taxonomy database of NCBI.

2.2   Sequence Analysis

Multiple sequence alignment was performed using ClustalW [11] . The sequence data was used to determine distances using DNADIST program of the Phylogeny Inference Package (PHYLIP)[12]. The Jukes-Cantor distance parameter was selected for determining evolutionary distances. Each sequence for all the datasets was mapped onto a 12-dimensional fuzzy vector i.e., each sequence was represented in terms of its fuzzy polynucleotide space. Distance matrices were computed using the NTV distance metric for the same sequences.

2.3   Phylogenetic Analysis

Neighbour Joining (NJ) method, one of the most effective distance based methods, was used for phylogenetic tree construction. The distance matrices generated through DNADIST and NTV metric served as input for the NEIGHBOR program of PHYLIP. Bootstrap values were set to 1000 for all trees.

Table 1. Different strains of Dengue type 3 used in this study

Strain/Isolate	Country*	Identifier	Accession Number
BID V1015	VNM	DEN_VNM1	EU482459
BID V1017	VNM	DEN_VNM2	EU482461
PF92/2986	FRN	DEN_FRN1	AY744683
PF89/320219	FRN	DEN_FRN2	AY744678

Table 1. (*Continued*)

PF89/27643	FRN	DEN_FRN3	AY744677
"ThD3_1283_98"	THN	DEN_THN1	AY676349
"C0360/94"	THN	DEN_THN2	AY923865
"ThD3_0104_93"	THN	DEN_THN3	AY676350
"ThD3_0055_93"	THN	DEN_THN4	AY676351
"C0331/94"	THN	DEN_THN5	AY876494
"BR DEN3 RO1-02"	BRZ	DEN_BRZ1	EF629370
"BR DEN3 290-02"	BRZ	DEN_BRZ2	EF629369
"BR DEN3 95-04"	BRZ	DEN_BRZ3	EF629366
"BR DEN3 97-04"	BRZ	DEN_BRZ4	EF629367
"BR74886/02"	BRZ	DEN_BRZ5	AY679147
DENV-3/VE/BID-V2484/2007	VZL	DEN_VZL1	FJ850111
DENV-3/VE/BID-V2480/2007	VZL	DEN_VZL3	FJ850109
DENV-3/VE/BID-V2455/2001	VZL	DEN_VZL4	FJ850098
DENV-3/VE/BID-V2452/2001	VZL	DEN_VZL5 ·	FJ850097
DENV-3/KH/BID-V2089/2006	CBD	DEN_CBD1	FJ639729
DENV-3/KH/BID-V2088/2005	CBD	DEN_CBD2	FJ639728
DENV-3/KH/BID-V2086/2005	CBD	DEN_CBD3	FJ639727
DENV-3/KH/BID-V2083/2004	CBD	DEN_CBD4	FJ639726
DENV-3/KH/BID-V2081/2003	CBD	DEN_CBD5	FJ639724
DENV-3/US/BID-V2119/2002	USA	DEN_USA1	FJ547082
DENV-3/US/BID-V2118/2001	USA	DEN_USA2	FJ547081
BDH02-7	BAN	DEN_BAN1	AY496877
BDH02-4	BAN	DEN_BAN2	AY496874
BDH02-3	BAN	DEN_BAN3	AY496873

*Countries are abbreviated as follows: Vietnam=VNM, France=FRN, Thailand=THN, Brazil=BRZ, Cambodia=CBD, United Stated of America=USA, Bangladesh=BAN, Venezuela=VZL.

Table 2. Members of the genus *Microbacterium* whose gyrB sequences were considered in this study

Species	Accession no
M.aerolatum	AM181475
M.arborescens	AM181476
M.aurantiacum	AM181477
M.aurum	AM181478
M.chocolatum	AM181479
M.dextranolyticum	AM181480
M.esteraromaticum	AM181481
M.flavescens	AM181482
M.foliorum	AM181483
M.hominis	AM181484
M.imperiale	AJ784798
M.keratanolyticum	AM181485
M.ketosireducens	AM181486
M.kitamiense	AM181487
M.lacticum	AM181488
M.liquefaciens	AM181489
M.laevaniformans	AM181490
M.luteolum	AM181491
M.maritypicum	AM181492
M.oxydans	AM181493
M.phyllosphaerae	AM181494
M.resistens	AM181495
M.saperdae	AM181496
M.schleiferi	AM181497
M.terregens	AM181498
M.testaceum	AM181499
M.thalassium	AM181500
Agromyces albus	AM181501

Table 3. Members whose cyt B sequences were considered in this study

Taxa	Species	Identifier
Class Mammalia	*Loxodonta cyclotis*	African forest elephant (f.elephant)
	Loxodonta africana	African Savanna elephant(s.elephant)
	Cynopterus horsfieldi	Bat
	Equus caballus	Horse
	Rhinoceros unicornis	Rhino
	Cavia porcellus	Guinea Pig
	Myoxus glis	Fat Dormouse
	Delphinus delphis	Dolphin

Table 3. (*Continued*)

	Kogia breviceps	Sperm Whale
	H.liberiensis	Hippo
	Bos taurus	Cow
	Cervus duvaucelii	Deer
Order Primates		
Hominoidea:Apes	*Homo sapiens*	Human
	Pan paniscus	Pygmy Chimp
	Gorilla gorilla gorilla	Western Gorilla
	Pongo pygmaeus	Orangutan
	Hylobates lar	Common Gibbon(Co-Gibbon)
	Hylobates gabriellae	Red-cheeked Gibbon
	Aotus lemurinus griseimembra	A.lemurinus
	Saimiri boliviensis boliviensis	S.boliviensis
	Eulemur fulvus albifrons	Lemur
Class Aves	*Buteo buteo*	Buzzard
	Phaethon rubricauda	Red-tailed tropic
Class Amphibia	*Xenopus laevis*	X.levis
	Bufo japonicus	Japanese toad
	Pelobates cultripes	Western spadefoot toad
Class Reptilia	*Typhlops reticulatus*	Worm Snake
	Naja naja	Cobra
Class Osteichthyes	*Parargyrops edita*	Parargyrops
	Tribolodon nakamurai	Bony Fish
Class Chondrichthyes	*Chimaera monstrosa*	Rabbit fish

3   Results

For all the datasets, there was a marked difference in the tree topologies for the trees constructed using the Jukes-Cantor distance and the NTV metric. The trees generated employing the Jukes-Cantor distance conformed to the observed phylogenetic relationships for all the datasets, while the NTV metric based trees showed varying results. Figure 1(a) and 1(b) represent the trees generated for dataset 1, employing the Jukes Cantor distance and the NTV metric respectively. As can be observed, the NTV metric fails to show distinct clusters for all the viral isolates from different countries.

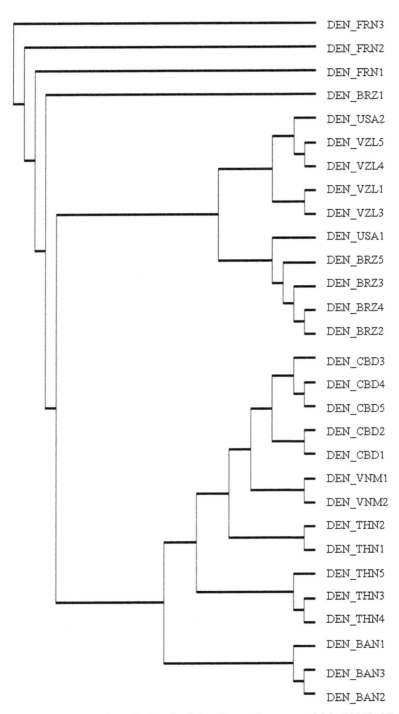

Fig. 1. (a). Tree constructed employing the Jukes-Cantor distance model in DNADIST using the NEIGHBOUR JOINING method for Dataset 1.

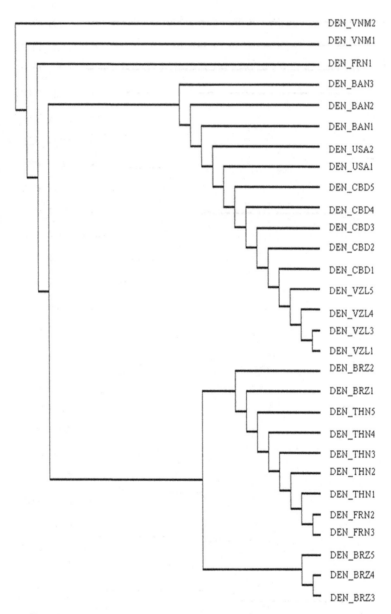

Fig.1 (b). Tree constructed employing the NTV distance metric and the NEIGHBOUR JOINING method for Dataset 1

Figures 2(a) and 2(b) reflect the difference in tree topologies for the trees generated using the Jukes Cantor distance and the NTV metric for Dataset 2. 2(a) conforms to established phylogeny of *Microbacterium* [13] , however the NTV based phylogenetic tree shows starkly contrasting results, and does not agree with the known phylogenetic relationship of the family. For example, the NTV metric classifies *M.arborescens* with *M.aerolatum*, while it is known to be evolutionarily closer to *M. imperiale* instead, as reflected by the Jukes-Cantor distance in 2(a). The established phylogeny of the Microbacterium genus follows distinct clusters, while the NTV-based tree shows incorrect and fewer clades of taxa.

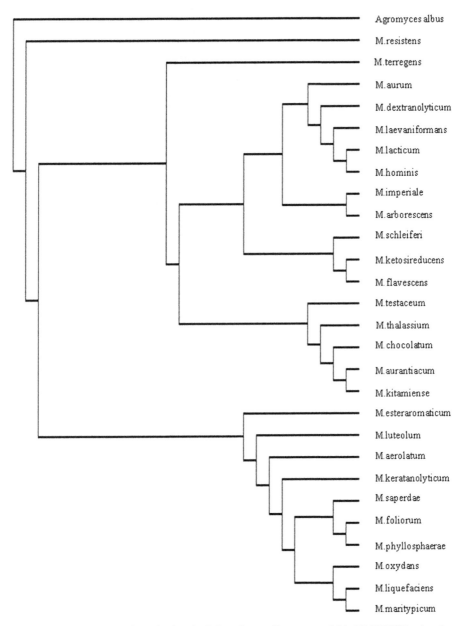

Fig. 2 (a). Tree constructed employing the Jukes-Cantor distance model in DNADIST using the NEIGHBOUR JOINING method for Dataset 2, using *Agromyces* as outgroup.

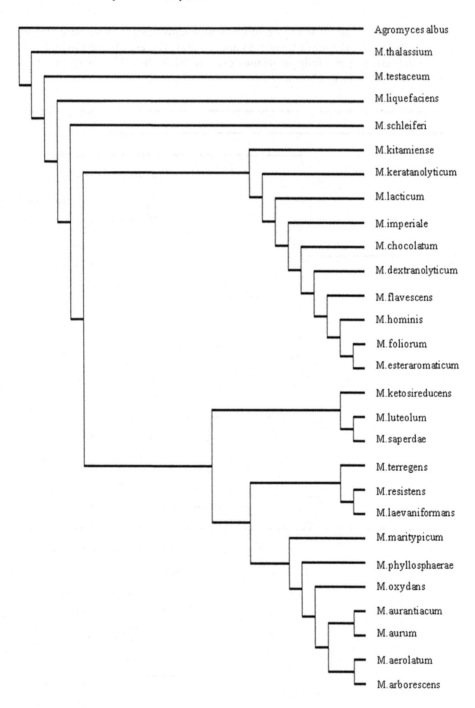

Fig. 2 (b). Tree constructed employing the NTV distance metric and NEIGHBOUR JOINING method for Dataset 2, using Agromyces as outgroup

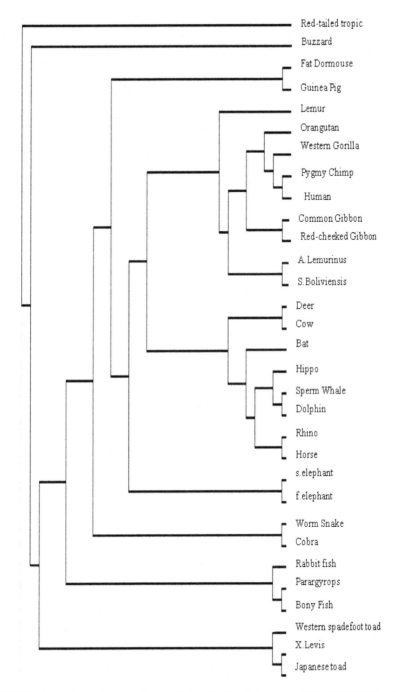

Fig. 3 (a). Tree constructed employing the Jukes-Cantor distance model in DNADIST using the NEIGHBOUR JOINING method for Dataset 3

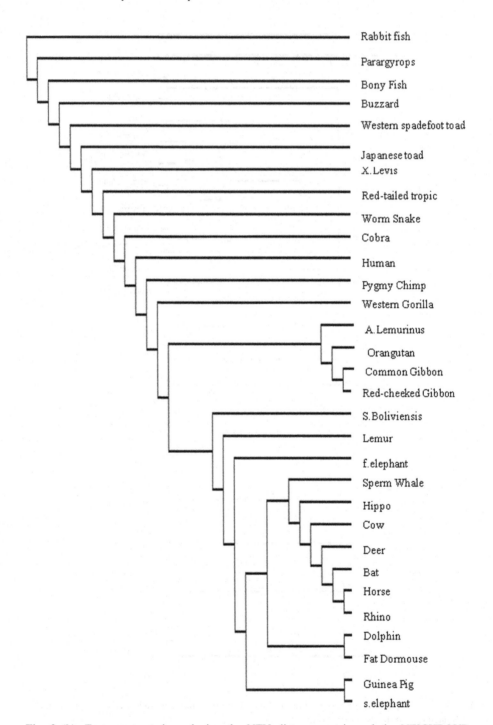

Fig. 3 (b). Tree constructed employing the NTV distance metric and the NEIGHBOUR JOINING method for Dataset 3.

Figures 3(a) and (b) similarly reflect the differences observed in the two methods of phylogenetic reconstruction for dataset 3. As can be observed, the NTV metric does not give distinct clusters for different members of the vertebrate classes. Also, it misclassifies African Savanna elephant with guinea pig, which otherwise belong to different classes. While the Gibbons are seen to cluster together in a single clade in both trees, the similarity between the generated trees is otherwise limited. These results are contrary to those seen in 3(a), and differ from the already proven taxonomic relationships in vertebrates. Further, cytochrome B sequences are highly conserved among eukaryotes, and are known to conform to different relationships among the data representatives. The NTV-metric could not correctly capture distances even among such well-documented similarities.

The same variation in tree topologies was seen for the phylogenetic trees constructed using the other six datasets for the two methods. NTV-based tree showed diametrically opposite results to the expected tree, based on known relationships. Further, in all cases, the number of distinct clades are significantly lower in the NTV-based trees as opposed to clear clusters observed in the Jukes-Cantor method based trees. This illuminates the limitation of the metric in capturing evolutionary relationships among various taxa. Thus, for all the datasets, the NTV metric failed to correctly represent the phylogenetic relationships among organisms.

4   Discussion

Some of the possible reasons for the failure of the fuzzy polynucleotide space in determining biological distances are as under:

Failure could be due to the observation that Fuzzy Polynucleotide Sequence is same for two different sequences, where one sequence is just a permutation of triplets of the other sequence, as suggested by K. Sadegh Zadeh [14]. The distance between these two sequences would be zero according to the NTV metric, whereas quite the opposite is true.

Another explanation for the limitation of the NTV metric in phylogeny is that phylogeny is a depiction of evolutionary distances between sequences, and takes into account per-site substitutions in a sequence alignment. The conventional distance based approaches used for phylogenetic construction employ distance parameters such as Jukes-Cantor distance, Kimura 2-point correction parameter etc. The Jukes-Cantor substitution model reflects the number of synonymous and non-synonymous substitutions per site of the alignment, and hence is a reflection of the number of changes occurred in DNA over the course of evolution. Since NTV is independent of sequence alignment, but rather depends on the relative base frequencies at each site of the codon, it does not account for evolutionary changes and hence is not an appropriate indicator of distances between biological sequences.

5   Concluding Remarks

The limited study infers that the fuzzy polynucleotide formalism may not be suitable in the construction of phylogenetic trees, as it is not a true indicator of distances among biological sequences.

Acknowledgements. The research reported in this sequel was carried out when the authors were with Bioinformatics Centre, Savitribai Phule Pune University, Pune India. The authors specially thank Dr. Urmila Kale for her constant encouragement.

References

1. Ohlsson, M., Schlosshauer, M.: A novel approach to local reliability of sequence alignments. Bioinformatics **18**(6), 847–854 (2002)
2. Cordón, O., Gomide, F., Herrera, F., Hoffmann, F., Magdalena, L.: Ten years of genetic fuzzy systems: current framework and new trends. Fuzzy Sets and Systems **141**(1), 5–31 (2004)
3. Belacel, N., Cuperlović-Culf, M., Laflamme, M., Ouellette, R.: Fuzzy J-Means and VNS methods for clustering genes frommicroarray data. Bioinformatics **20**(11), 1690–1701 (2004)
4. Bandyopadhyay, S.: An efficient technique for superfamily classification of amino acid sequences: feature extraction, fuzzy clustering and prototype selection. Fuzzy Sets and Systems **152**(1), 5–16 (2005)
5. Sadegh-Zadeh, K.: Fuzzy genomes. Artif. Intell. Med. **18**, 1–28 (2000)
6. Torres, A., Nieto, J.J.: The fuzzy polynucleotide space: Basic properties. Bioinformatics **19**(5), 587–592 (2003)
7. Kosko, B.: Neural Networks and Fuzzy Systems. Prentice-Hall, Englewood Cliffs (1992)
8. Torres, A., Nieto, J.J.: Fuzzy Logic in Medicine and Bioinformatics. Journal of Biomedicine and Biotechnology **2006**, 1–7 (2006)
9. Georgiou, D.N., Karakasidis, T.E., Nieto, J.J., Torres, A.: Use of fuzzy clustering technique and matrices to classify amino acids and its impact to Chou's pseudo amino acid composition. Journal of Theoretical Biology **257**, 17–26 (2009)
10. Torres, A., Nieto, J.J.: Comments on "The fuzzy polynucleotide space revisited" by Kazem Sadegh-Zadeh. Artificial Intelligence in Medicine **41**, 81–82 (2007)
11. Larkin, M.A., et al.: Clustal W and Clustal X version 2.0. Bioinformatics **23**(21), 2947–2948 (2007)
12. Felsenstein, J.: PHYLIP (Phylogeny Inference Package) version 3.6. Distributed by the author. Department of Genome Sciences, University of Washington, Seattle (2005)
13. Richert, K., Brambilla, E., Stackebrandt, E.: The phylogenetic significance of peptidoglycan types: molecular analysis of the genera Microbacterium and Aureobacterium based upon sequence comparison of gyrB, rpoB, recA and ppk and 16SrRNA genes. Syst. Appl. Microbiol. **30**, 102–108 (2006)
14. Sadegh-Zadeh, K.: The Fuzzy Polynucleotide Space Revisited. Artificial Intelligence in Medicine **41**, 69–80 (2007)

An Overview of Semantically-Based TCM Telemedicine Systems

[1] HerbMiners Informatics Limited, Unit 209A, 2/F Photonics Centre, Phase One, Hong Kong Science and Technology Park, Pak Shek Kok, Tai Po, NT, Hong Kong
{iamjackei,wilfred.lin}@gmail.com
[2] Department of Computing, The Hong Kong Polytechnic University, Hung Hom, Kowloon, Hong Kong
{iamjackei,wilfred.lin}@gmail.com

Abstract. Traditional Chinese Medicine (TCM) is gaining its popularity in recent years. The limited exchange of medical knowledge due to geographical constraints etc. will be disadvantageous to patients. It is crucial to capture the knowledge and experience in a computer-based representation. With the application of semantic network and ontology, knowledge and experience will then be kept and stored in a semantic manner, which facilitates effective and efficient knowledge exchange and sharing.

Keywords: Semantic network · Ontology · Telemedicine · Traditional Chinese Medicine

1 Introduction

The knowledge of Traditional Chinese Medicine (TCM) has existed for more than 3000 years till now, while TCM practices are in various forms according to different geographical and environmental constraints. The exchange of medical knowledge and clinical experience was limited due to transportation difficulties, language barriers etc. As times go by, the stored medical information has been gradually refine to constitute more than 5000 pieces of works in extant. Useful herbal ingredients including plant parts, minerals and animal matter have been added and incorporated into the conceptual TCM pharmacopeia.

Traditional Chinese Medicine (TCM) has been widely used for many centuries in China, it is gaining more and more adoption all over the world. The trends in the use of TCM will be aided by standard and uniform vocabulary and an agreed consensus by the domain expert, it is crucial to capture the underlying clinical TCM body of knowledge and practices in a computer-based representation. This has a semantic basis in which the focus is on the meaning of the knowledge but not the syntactic format of its representation. Ontology will be utilized as well to make the knowledge more readily searchable and queried.

2 TCM and Telemedicine

One of the earliest definitions of the notion of Telemedicine can be found in the publication [Lacroix99]. It refers to make use of the Internet to deliver medical care to every corner all over the world. Thus, those web-based medical system has at least

© IFIP International Federation for Information Processing 2015
T. Dillon (Ed.): IFIP AI 2015, IFIP AICT 465, pp. 17–25, 2015.
DOI: 10.1007/978-3-319-25261-2_2

some telemedicine elements, independent of its scale. Telemedicine systems can be broadly divided into different types, according to their goals and functions as follows:

a)   Curative Systems – medical practitioners use the system to achieve the diagnosis and treatment goals.

b)   Consultative Systems – through the system interface the user can obtain needed information, such as information about named patent drugs, and addresses/expertise of medical practitioners in the region/vicinity.

c)   Medical Information Management Systems in terms of data storage and retrieval (e.g. medical images).

d)   Decision Support Systems – this happens in various forms, for example, the physician, who is using a telemedicine system (e.g. the PuraPharm's D/P (diagnosis/prescription) system in a mobile clinic [JWong09] may import biometric reports to aid the diagnostic decision/precision as shown by Fig. 1.

Fig. 1. Imported information to aid diagnosis

The aim of doing this is to let people including non-medical domain expert and registered medical personnel consult and verify knowledge if necessary from the knowledge base. Yet, a knowledge base can be for a general purpose and similar to a dictionary in this sense. It also help experts to clarify doubts due to multi-representations owing to disparate national or regional conceptions of a medical phenomenon. A typical example in the Western/allopathic medicine area is the UMLS (Unified Medical Language System [UMLS]), which was developed by the US National Library of Medicine to resolve the differences in Western/allopathic clinical terminology due to regional and/or national disparities. The UMLS is ontology-based. Another ontology-based system is the disease and treatment ontology for Western Allopathic Medicine [Hadzic05 and Hadzic10]. By its nature the UMLS is not for frontline clinical application to allow computer-aided diagnosis and treatment in contrast to the PuraPharm's TCM (Traditional Chinese Medicine) telemedicine mobile clinic (MC) system. The UMLS is consultative in nature. That is, it is not a clinical system but a consultation setup that people can interact with to sort out terminology problems. Therefore, its aim is to provide an interactive learning, reference, and bridging mechanism for knowledge gaps in a global sense. For example, in conventional/Western/allopathic medicine different countries may have different definitions for an observed phenomenon. In order to resolve the similarity and differences of various definitions, as well as language peculiarities on a global scale, meta-thesauri can serve as an effective means as shown by the UMLS.

3   Explicit and Implicit Semantics

If a single statement composed of a string pattern which can induce various interpretations for different people with different perspectives, the semantics of this string is then considered implicit. This is similar to deciphering the embedded logic in a given program without its original detailed specification. The logical representation can vary from one interpreter to another. For example, the hierarchy represented in the UML (Unified Modeling Language) style in Fig. 2 can result in ambiguous interpretations (i.e. semantics) from different people for the "logical points" a and b, which can be logically AND or OR; vice versa; or EXLUSIVE OR, leading to unexpected results. For curative medicine, this kind of logical freedom is disadvantageous to the patients. For this reason the semantics in the ontology must be explicitly defined by the principle of "single meaning for every semantic path".

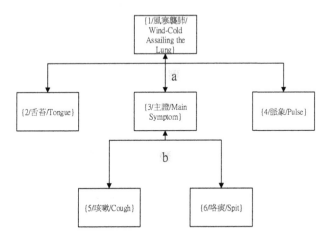

Fig. 2. Implicit logical representation – implicit semantics (bilingual)

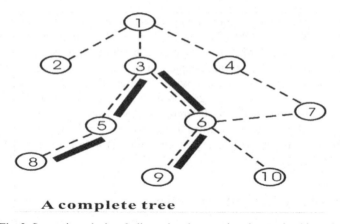

A complete tree

Fig. 3. Semantic paths in a 3-dimensional semantic subsumption hierarchy

The 3-dimensional subsumption hierarchy in Fig. 3 contains many operations or semantic paths (e.g. {3,5,8} and {3,6,9}). Yet, from a 2-dimensional viewpoint Fig. 2 is simply a network representation of many possible operational paths (i.e. traversal paths) between any two points. To create an operational ontology-based system (with a mini-ontology) out of this tree, it is necessary to elaborate this 2-dimensional view into a 3-dimensional one. Then, the focus is represented by the chosen "lead", which in reality is the first point where the parsing mechanism begins to process. For example, if node 1 is the chosen lead for parsing in Fig. 3, then the possible 14 semantic paths for the 3-dimensional subsumption hierarchy are the following: {1,2}; {1,3}; {1,3,5}; {1,3,5,8}; {1,3,6}; {1,3,6,9}; {1,3,6,10}; {1,4}; {1,4,7}; {1,4,7,6}; (1,4,7,6,9}; and {1,4,7,6,10}. If every semantic path is supported by only a single dedicated software module/object, then the meanings of the set of semantic paths (represented by the equal number of software modules or objects) form the lexicon for this particular system. As a result, the system always gives a clear, consistent and unambiguous (i.e. explicit) answer to every query, which is another form of a semantic path in the lexicon. Although the semantic paths in the lexicon are explicit, every query is constructed "implicitly" or with user-transparency according to the input sequence of the atomic elements. In fact, the semantic paths can be further classified into more specific semantic groups for various goals, similar in fashion to the conceptual UMLS framework.

4   Ontology-Based TCM Telemedicine System – Major Aspects

The focus of this paper is to give an overview of the semantic TCM telemedicine system. The following aspects should be addressed:

a)   Ontology Modelling
b)   Ontology Implementation Tool
c)   Internet Capability

d)   Cross-layer Logical Transitivity
e)   Automatic System Generation
f)   Pervasive Support
g)   Ontology Evolution

4.1   Ontology Modelling

The design of the system begins with the ontology model blueprint layout followed by the consensus certification. The ontology includes the whole or part of the formalisms and knowledge in the relevant domain. In this sense, an ontology-based system is data/knowledge oriented. This model should be understandable by both TCM domain experts and system developers so as to facilitate evaluation and critiquing of the ontology by the domain experts for correctness and completeness.

4.2   Ontology Implementation Tool

The tool is usually a high level language, which can correlate all the concepts in the ontology into a logical subsumption hierarchy. The ontology modelling blueprint is mainly for human understanding, and the embedded subsumption hierarchy should be translated meticulously into the corresponding semantic network for machine understanding/processing/execution. Therefore, it is necessary to choose a tool that has the support of "ontology model blueprint-to-semantic-net translation". It is better for the conversion process to be automatic [JWong08b]. In this light, the languages (or metadata models/systems) proposed by W3C (World Wide Web Consortium) [W3Ca, W3Cb], namely, XML (Extensible Mark-up Language), RDF (Resource Description Framework), and OWL (Web Ontology Language) are good to choose from, as they have widespread automatic translation support.

4.3   Internet Capability

Telemedicine relies on the Internet to achieve different goals on the web. For example, the telemedicine system may send out analysts or data-miners to search the web for necessary information to support the system's ontology evolution – the concept of a living ontology [JWong08a, WLin13, AWong15]. This is well exemplified by the 2nd generation of the PuraPharm D/P (diagnosis/prescription) telemedicine system that supports the YOT (a charitable organization in Hong Kong) mobile clinics in Hong Kong. These mobile clinics have been treating thousands of patients weekly in recent years.

4.4   Cross-Layer Logical Transitivity

A practical telemedicine system should have a 3-layer architecture. These three layers are as follows:

- Bottom Layer – the knowledge/database that embeds the subsumption hierarchy that represents the logical relationships among the physical data items/entities included in the consensus-certified ontology.
- Middle Layer – this subsumption hierarchy is also realized in the middle layer as the semantic network for machine understanding and execution.
- Top Layer – the query system that implements the ontology for user under-standing and manipulation.

The three layers are logically clones of one another, and therefore they should have cross-layer semantic transitivity. With this transitivity any entity in any layer should have corresponding representations in the other two layers.

It is useful to compare the TCM Curative and Decision Support System with the 3 Layer Architecture of the UMLS consultation system. The UMLS is ontology-based and has three distinctive layers: i) the modularized query system (the modules are semantic groups) at the top level, ii) the middle logical semantic-net layer, which was constructed from the semantics embedded in the information of the bottom onto-logical layer, and iii) the bottom ontology is integrated by nature and normally has a subsumption hierarchy of various sub-ontologies of different origins [Gruber93a, Gruber93b, Guarino95].

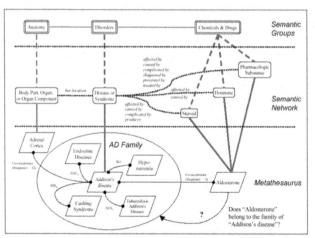

Overview of the methodology applied to the relationships of "Aldosterone" to "Addison's disease"

Fig. 4. The 3-layer UMLS hierarchy [UMLS]

There is, therefore, some similarity between the overall structures of the two sys-tems even though one is used for Curative and Decision Support Purposes whilst this is used as a consultation system.

4.5   Automatic System Generation

Cross-layer semantic transitivity can be achieved correctly by automatic system generation or customization (ASG/C). This approach is a new software engineering paradigm, which requires the user to provide the ontology blueprint layout. With support of the master ontology, where the ontology specification is either a part or the whole of it, the ASG/C mechanism generates/customizes the final ontology-based system in one shot.

4.6   Pervasive Support

A telemedicine system requires the support of a wireless-based pervasive computing infrastructure (PCI), which maintains the smart space for the collaborating systems. In the PuraPharm mobile clinic environment, the collaborating systems are the mobile clinics. The essence of the PCI support is better explained by using the successful PuraPharm's mobile clinic (MC) based telemedicine D/P (diagnosis/prescription) system depicted in Fig. 5. The PCI maintains the smart space, which is each occupied by a mobile clinic. The mobile clinic then communicates with the central system, as well as its peers, via the wireless means provided by the PCI. The MC operation is semi-autonomous because the physician can treat the patient at the spot, but the case history of the patient may have to be downloaded from the central computer that runs the fast network. The MC has to inform the central system of its updated local drug inventory. The central system also collects the necessary MC statistics on-line for proactive planning and action. If the MC physician needs help in the diagnostic process, the central system would solicit the relevant information from other friendly sites via the Internet.

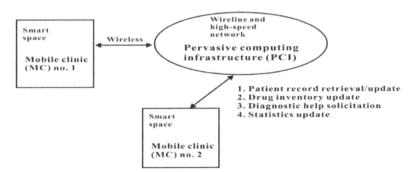

Fig. 5. A PuraPharm's pervasive MC-based telemedicine D/P system

4.7   Ontology Evolution Approach

It is important that the TCM ontology keeps itself updated from time to time by taking into account the new knowledge and insights that are being generated as time passes. It should be able to absorb information from every fresh case into the "master" ontology as new knowledge. In this light, this master ontology is a living and evolving system.

Hence, it is clear that there is a need for a framework of ontology evolution for the TCM ontology so that it reflects the new knowledge and insights. To achieve ontology evolution, we need to:

- Ascertain the new knowledge
- Represent this potential new knowledge temporarily in a form compatible with the ontology
- Carryout consensus certification of this new potential new knowledge
- Enhancing the master ontology only with the consensus certified portions of the new knowledge

In order to ascertain the new knowledge, a text mining approach will be utilized. The data and text mining approach suggests potential changes to the TCM ontology. A temporary representation of these potential changes is stored in a part of the master aliasing table. The proposed potential changes to the ontology are then subject to consensus certification by a panel of TCM domain experts, and only those changes that are approved by this consensus certification are then included into the master TCM ontology through the master aliasing table.

5   Conclusion

This paper discussed an overview of semantically-based TCM telemedicine systems. The underlying principles of such a TCM telemedicine system were briefly explored. The proposed future work is to apply the technique of deep learning and predictive analysis for diagnosis/prescription differentiation recommendations.

References

1. Wong, A.K.Y., Wong, J.H.K., Lin, W.W.K., Dillon, T.S., Chang, E.: Semantically Based Clinical TCM Telemedicine Systems. Studies in Computational Intelligence, vol. 587, pp. 1–152. Springer (2015). ISBN 978-3-662-46023-8
2. Gruber, T.R.: A Translation Approach to Portable Ontology Specification. Knowledge Acquisition 5(2), 199–220 (1993)
3. Gruber, T.R.: Toward principles for the design of ontologies used for knowledge sharing. In: Proceedings of the International Workshop on Formal Ontology in Conceptual Analysis and Knowledge Representation, Padova, Italy, March 17, 1993
4. Guarino, N., Giaretta, P.: Ontologies and Knowledge Bases: Towards a Terminological Clarification. Towards Very Large Knowledge Bases: Knowledge Building and Knowledge Sharing, 25–32 (1995)
5. Hadzic, M., Chang, E.: Medical ontologies to support human disease research and control. International Journal of Web and Grid Service, Inderscience (2005)
6. Hadzic, M., Wongthongtham, P., Dillon, T., Chang, E.: Ontology-based Multi-agent Systems, 274p. Springer Publications, Germany (2010). ISBN 978-3-642-01903-6

7. Wong, J.H.K., Dillon, T.S., Wong, A.K.Y., Lin, W.W.K.: Text mining for real-time ontology evolution. In: Data Mining for Business Applications, pp. 143–150. Springer (2008). ISBN: 978-0-387-79419-8

8. Wong, J.H., Lin, W.W., Wong, A.K., Dillon, T.S.: An ontology supported meta-interface for the development and installation of customized web based telemedicine systems. In: Brinkschulte, U., Givargis, T., Russo, S. (eds.) SEUS 2008. LNCS, vol. 5287, pp. 233–244. Springer, Heidelberg (2008)

9. Wong, J.H.K., Lin, W.W.K., Wong, A.K.Y., Dillon, T.S.: TCM (Traditional Chinese Medicine) telemedicine with enterprise ontology support – a form of consensus-certified collective human intelligence. In: Proceedings of the International Conference on Industrial Technology (ICIT). Monash University, Victoria, Australia, February 10-13, 2009

10. Lacroix, A., Lareng, L., Rossignol, G., Padeken, D., Bracale, M., Ogushi, Y., Wootton, R., Sanders, J., Preost, S., McDonald, I.: G-7 Global Healthcare Applications Sub-project 4. Telemedicine Journal, March 1999

11. UMLS. http://umls.nlm.nih.gov/

12. W3C, Ontology Definition MetaModel (2005). http://www.omg.org/docs/ad/05-08-01.pdf#search='Ontology%20Definition%20Metamodel

13. W3C, Web Service Architecture (Working Paper). http://www.w3.org/TR/ws-arch/

14. Lin, W.W.K., Wong, J.H.K.: Artificial neural network based chinese medicine diagnosis in decision support manner and herbal ingredient discoveries. In: Data Analytics for Traditional Chinese Medicine Research, pp. 123–132. Springer (2012)

Teenagers' Stress Detection Based on Time-Sensitive Micro-blog Comment/Response Actions

Liang Zhao, Jia Jia, and Ling Feng[✉]

Department of Computer Science and Technology, Tsinghua University,
Beijing 100084 , China
zhaoliang0415@gmail.com, {jjia,fengling}@tsinghua.edu.cn

Abstract. Accurately detecting psychological stress in time is a significant issue in the modern stressful society, especially for adolescents who are not mature enough to cope with pressure well. Micro-blog offers a new channel for teens' stress detection, since more and more teenagers nowadays prefer to express themselves on the lively virtual social networks. Previous work mainly rely on tweeting contents to detect tweeters' psychological stress. However, a tweet is limited to 140 characters, which are too short to provide enough information to accurately figure out its tweeter's stress. To overcome the limitation, this paper proposes to leverage details of social interactions between tweeters and their following friends (i.e., time-sensitive comment/response actions under a tweet) to aid stress detection. Experimental results through a real user study show that time sensitivity of comment/response acts plays a significant role in stress detection, and involving such interaction acts can improve the detection performance by 23.5% in F-measure over that without such interactions.

1 Introduction

The increasingly faster life pace in the competitive society often makes people stressful, especially for teenagers who are too immature to deal with psychological pressures. Currently, 20% teenagers have psychological illness around the world [2]. An online survey of 1018 U.S. teens (aged 13-17) made by the American Psychological Association in August, 2013 found that teens suffered stress in all areas of their lives, from school to friends, work and family, which negatively affected every aspect of their lives, and about 27% of the teens experienced extreme stress and 55% experienced moderate stress in the past school year [4]. If such pressures cannot get properly relieved in time, the teenagers will suffer severe physical and mental problems under accumulated pressures, such as clinical depressions, insomnia, and even committing suicide. According to China Center for Disease Control and Prevention [1], suicide has become the top cause of death among Chinese youth, and excessive stress is considered to be a major factor of suicide. Also in Korea, suicide has become teenagers' No.1 killer in

© IFIP International Federation for Information Processing 2015
T. Dillon (Ed.): IFIP AI 2015, IFIP AICT 465, pp. 26–36, 2015.
DOI: 10.1007/978-3-319-25261-2_3

the past two years [3]. Annual increase of adolescent suicide rate has become a world-wide common problem.

As adolescence is a critical period for one's growth and development, it has significant value to pay attention to teenagers' psychological status and discover their suffering pressures in time. With the popularity of social networks, micro-blog offers another low-cost sensing channel to analyze teenagers' psychological pressures through their tweets, since more and more teenagers turn to micro-blog for information acquisition, personal interaction, self-expression, and emotion release. Some research work has already made efforts to detect user's stress and depression through micro-blog by analyzing their tweeting behaviors [8,9,13,15,18]. Leveraging tweeting contents such as linguistic and visual features to analyze user's stress has been proven feasible [11,16]. However, a tweet faces the limitation of only 140 characters, which is too short to provide enough content information to figure out stress and sometimes users may not express their stress so directly. To address the limitation, we propose to further involve comment/response acts under the tweet (comments, responses, likes and forwards) to better supplement stress detection. Such interactions are attached with unique timestamps. Considering time sensitivity, we select the interactions within a certain time gap right after the tweet is posted and construct a time-sensitive feature space for stress detection together with content of the tweet. Based on [16], we combine the content of both the tweet and time-sensitive comment/response acts under the tweet to extract content features for the four stress categories (academic, affection, interpersonal, self-cognition), respectively. From the observations that stressful tweets often receive more comments from friends, especially comments with care, comfort and encourage, and the psychological study [5] that users get inactive when suffering stress, we extract several novel interacting behavior features such as effective comment rate, reply rate, effective reply rate, and average interaction depth to help improve the stress detection. Our user study of 36 high school teenagers shows that time sensitivity of comment/response acts plays a significant role in stress detection and such acts in 30 minutes after the tweet posted are proved to be the most effective. Involving such interaction acts improves the detection performance by 23.5%.

To the best of our knowledge, this is the first work combining tweet contents and time-sensitive comment/response acts under the tweet for stress detection. There are also no previous stress detection work, specifying features for different stress categories.

The remainder of the paper is organized as follows. We review the related work in Section 2. Section 3 analyzes and extracts features from time-sensitive comment/response acts for teens' stress detection. Experimental performance through a real user study is evaluated in Section 4. Finally, we conclude the paper in Section 5.

2 Related Work

Computer-aided sentiment analysis and applications in social network has drawn much attention in recent years [10,11,16,19]. Many studies focus on the single tweet, leveraging content features such as text-based linguistic attributes and visual factors such as emoticons and images. [20] proposed a system called *Moodlens* to do sentiment analysis for Chinese Weibo via emoticons in tweets. The emoticons are divided into four different sentiment categories (i,e, angry, disgusting, joyful and sad), and a fast Naive Bayes classifiers works for the sentiment analysis of tweets.

Beside the content features, simple social interaction attributes are also involved. [12] proposed to detect user's psychological stress from social media via a deep convolution network on sequential time series in a certain time period. Simple social features like the number of -mentions, -replies, comments and likes are considered. User-level social connections such as (mutually) follow relationships and (mutually) -mentioned relationships were also investigated in [14] to improve sentiment analysis in Twitter. [17] explored comments to help predict emotions expressed by images posted on Flickr. However, time sensitivity of such social interaction attributes is not considered in these work.

The most closest related work is [11,16]. Focusing on the four main kinds of stress (*academic, affection, interpersonal* and *self-cognition*) that troubles teenagers, [16] extracted different features from teenagers' tweets, such as negative emotion words, negative emoticons, unusual post time and post frequency, etc., and several classifiers were leveraged to learn the potential stress category and corresponding stress level (0-5) behind the tweet. However, [16] only considered the content and unusual posting behavior of the tweet, ignoring social interactions such as comments and replies under the tweet. Besides, the detection process only returns one stress category and one level for a single tweet, but actually a single tweet may express several kinds of stress with different levels. [11] designed a deep sparse neural network to detect stress for arbitrary micro-blog users, using content features of the tweet including linguistic attributes as [16], visual attribute like color theme, brightness, etc, and simple social attributes like number of comments, retweets and favorites. they do consider the social factors, but ignore the details such as content of comments and the interaction of friends' comments and author's reply under the tweet . They only detected whether the user suffers stress, but did not quantitatively measure the stress level. Similarly, [11] also returned one stress category for one single tweet. In addition, for both the two work, content features are not category-specified and features are all static, no time-sensitive factor considered.

3   Stress Detection with Time-Sensitive Comment/Response Acts

Before introducing the details of stress detection, we first illustrate some notations used in the following of the paper by Table 1. And without loss of generality, we use interaction acts and comment/response acts interchangeably in the rest of the paper. Given a tweet $p = T_w(u, t_0, cont, SI^{\Delta t})$, four kinds of interaction acts under p constitute $SI^{\Delta t}$, comments, likes, and forwards from friends, as well as user's responses. When Δt is big enough, then $SI^{\Delta t}$ contains all the comments, replies, likes and forwards under p.

As in [16], let $\mathcal{C}_{ategory}=\{academic,\ affection, interpersonal, self\text{-}cognition\}$ be the set of teenagers' stress categories involved in the study, and $\mathcal{L}_{evel}=\{null,$ $light,\ moderate, strong\}$ be the set of stress levels, where $null$ means no-stress. For a single tweet p, we leverage time-sensitive interaction acts $SI^{\Delta t}$ together with content of p to form a feature space. Exploiting classification methods, the stress detection result of p is represented as $Stress(p) = ((C_i, Lv_1), \ldots, (C_4, Lv_4))$, where $C_i \in \mathcal{C}_{ategory}$ and $Lv_i \in \mathcal{L}_{evel}$. If $\forall Lv_i = null$ ($i = 1, \ldots, 4$), then $Stress(p)$ is a zero vector and p is a non-stressful tweet. Without loss of generality, we call those tweets with non-zero stress vector *stressful posts*.

Table 1. Notations covered in tweets

Notation	Representation	Description
p	$p = T_w(u, t_0, cont, SI^{\Delta t})$	A tweet posted by user u at time t_0 with the content of *cont*, and set of time-sensitive interactions acts $SI^{\Delta t}$ during $[t_0, t_0 + \Delta t]$
F	$F = \{f \mid f \text{ is a friend of } u\}$	Friend set of user u
c	$c = comm(f, t_c, cont, p), f \in F$	A comment from f at time t_c under tweet p, and *cont* is the content of the comment
r	$r = rep(u, t_r, c, cont, p)$	u's reply to comment c at time t_r under tweet p, and *cont* is the content of the reply
lk	$lk = like(f, t_l, p), f \in F$	Friend f puts a *like* seal on p at t_l
fw	$fw = fwrd(f, t_f, p), f \in F$	Friend f forwards p at time t_f
$C_{omm}(f, p, \Delta t)$	$= \{c \mid c.t_c \in [t_0, t_0 + \Delta t]\}$	Set of comments from f within Δt
$R_{ep}(u, f, p, \Delta t)$	$= \{r \mid r.t_r \in [t_0, t_0 + \Delta t]\}$	Set of replies to f within Δt
$L_{ikes}(F, p, \Delta t)$	$= \{lk \mid \forall f \in F, lk.t_l \in [t_0, t_0 + \Delta t]\}$	Set of likes within Δt
$F_{wrds}(F, p, \Delta t)$	$= \{fw \mid \forall f \in F, fw.t_f \in [t_0, t_0 + \Delta t]\}$	Set of forwards of p within Δt

3.1   Modified Content Features

A tweet is only 140 characters limited which is too short to provide enough content information to figure out stress and sometimes users are not likely to express their stress so directly via a brief tweet. Through daily observations, content of the communication between the user and his/her friends under the tweet provides powerful cues to help analyze stress. We consider the content of user interactions with friends (i.e., comments from friends and the user's replies) as part of the tweet to supplement more content information. Assume the combined content of p is denoted as

$$CCont(p, \Delta t) = \bigcup_{f \in F} \{c.cont, r.cont \mid c \in C_{omm}(f, p, \Delta t), r \in R_{ep}(u, f, p, \Delta t)\} \bigcup p.cont$$

Particularly, interactive comments and responses between user u and friend f are closely related in content and constitute a dialog. We take the content of dialog as a whole, and regard it as an item piece of $CCont(p, \Delta t)$. For each item piece in $CCont(p, \Delta t)$, we leverage a graph-based Chinese parser [6,7] to analyze linguistic associations, including the correspondence between stress categories and negative emotion words, and the grammatical relation between adverbs of degree and the modified negative emotion words, etc. A single tweet may convey several kinds of stress at the same time. Thus, for each stress category in $\mathcal{C}_{ategory}$, we specify content features from $CCont(p, \Delta t)$ as in [16]. i.e., number of negative emotion words, number of positive and negative emoticons, number of exclamation and question marks, emotional degree, etc.

3.2   Time-Sensitive Comment/Response Features

Comment/Response acts under a tweet is time-sensitive especially when the user is suffering from stress. For example, when a user posts a tweet expressing depression, his/her friends will always make in-time comments within a short time gap after the tweet is released. We select the interaction acts under the tweet p within $[t_0, t_0 + \Delta t]$ to extract the comment/response features.

Commenting Features from Crowd. Comments, likes and forwards are basic commenting features and always show the social attention to a tweet.

Number of Comments from Friends. The set of all the comments under the tweet p within $[t_0, t_0 + \Delta t]$ is

$$C_{omments}(F, p, \Delta t) = \bigcup_{f \in F} C_{omm}(f, p, \Delta t)$$

Number of Likes. People always put a *like* seal on a tweet to show their positive emotion or attitude to the tweet. Compared with those positive tweets, stressful tweets (negative tweets) obtain much less *likes*, even no *like*. We take the number of *likes* under a tweet as an indicator of potential stress, denoted as $|L_{ikes}(F, p, \Delta t)|$.

Number of Forwards. Users tend to forward public information such as news, advertisements and jokes, and seldom retweet personalized stressful tweets of another user. So stressful tweets enjoy less possibility to be forwarded by friends. The number of forwards here is denoted as $|F_{wrds}(F, u, p, \Delta t)|$.

Number of Effective Comments. Among all the comments from friends, we further check the details of the comments and distinguish those containing care, comfort, or encourage (e.g., "What's up?", "Don't worry", "Everything will be OK", or *hug* emoticon, etc.). Such comments are considered as *effective comments*. The set of effective comments under tweet p is denoted as $EC_{omments}(F, p, \Delta t)$. A lexicon with 132 such Chinese phrases, sentences and emoticons is constructed to identify effective comments. A tweet with more effective comments is more likely to be stressful.

Effective Comment Rate.(short for ECR, denoted as $ECR(F, p, \Delta t)$) is calculated as

$$ECR(F, p, \Delta t) = \frac{|EC_{omments}(F, p, \Delta t)|}{|C_{omments}(F, p, \Delta t)| + 1}$$

where $|(\cdot)|$ stands for the number of items in set $(\cdot)$ and we smooth the equation by adding 1 upon denominator. Obviously, a higher ECR denotes a bigger probability that the tweet is stressful.

Particularly, with any two of the three features (number of comments/effective comments and effective comment rate) we can deduce the other one. Thus, for commenting features we can choose any two.

Replying Features of the User. Besides the social behaviors of the crowd (friends), behaviors of the user himself also make sense in stress detection. Psychological study [5] shows that a user in stress may perform low activeness in social networks. Such inactiveness can be revealed from user's reactions to the comments from friends. Three features corresponding to the user's replying behaviors are identified.

Reply Rate. If a user is absorbed in big stress, s/he tends to be inactive, which can be revealed from his/her activeness of reply to the comments. The reply rate (short for RR, denoted as $RR(u, p, \Delta t)$) is calculated by the rate of replies over total number of comments. Assume $R_{eplies}(u, F, p, \Delta t) = \bigcup_{f \in F} R_{ep}(u, f, p, \Delta t)$ is the set of user replies to all the friends under p, then

$$RR(u, p, \Delta t) = \frac{|R_{eplies}(u, F, p, \Delta t)|}{|C_{omments}(F, p, \Delta t)| + 1}$$

A lower reply rate suggests that the user is not so active and it is highly possible that s/he is suffering stress. Similarly, among the three features (number of comments/replies, and reply rate), we can deduce the other one with any two.

Effective Reply Rate. Effective replies are those responses to the effective comments. The set of effective replies under p within $[t_0, t_0 + \Delta t]$ is

$$ER_{eplies}(u, F, p, \Delta t) = \{r | r.c \in EC_{omments}(F, p, \Delta t), r.t_r \in [t_0, t_0 + \Delta t]\}$$

We measure the effective reply rate (short for ERR, denoted as $ERR(p, \Delta t)$) by the proportion of effective reply over the total number of effective comments.

$$ERR(p, \Delta t) = \frac{|ER_{eplies}(u, F, p, \Delta t)|}{|EC_{omments}(F, p, \Delta t)| + 1}$$

Average Interaction Depth with Friends. A friend may comment multiple times under the same tweet, and the user may also make corresponding replies. Then, such interaction between them constitutes a dialog. In the dialog, once a new comment-reply pair comes, the interaction depth between the friend and the user accordingly increases by 1. Assume a friend f and the user u make a comment-reply dialog under tweet p, then the interaction depth between f and u in tweet p within $[t_0, t_0 + \Delta t]$ is calculated as

$$iDep(f, u, p, \Delta t) = min(|C_{omm}(f, p, \Delta t)|, |R_{ep}(u, f, p, \Delta t)|)$$

For all the friends who comment the tweet, the average interaction depth is computed by

$$avg\_iDep(F, u, p, \Delta t) = \frac{1}{|F|} \sum_{f \in F} iDep(f, u, p, \Delta t)$$

The average interaction depth reveals the user's activeness as well. The smaller the average interaction depth is, the less active the user performs, so that s/he has a higher risk of stress suffered.

4   Experimental Study

4.1   Setup

Psychological stress detection is a highly personalized issue and there are no available benchmark specially for the problem. In this work, we collect data ourselves and conduct a user study on a real micro-blog data set. 36 high school students (15 males and 21 females, aged between 15 and 17) in Shaanxi Province, China, participated in the user study. 21,648 tweets from 2013/1/1 to 2015/5/1 were collected from their accounts in Tencent Weibo[1], averagely 636 tweets per teenager. Recalling the real situations, they were asked to scan their own tweets one by one and annotated the psychological stress on the four stress categories in $\mathcal{C}_{category}$ and corresponding stress levels in $\mathcal{L}_{evel}$ expressed in each single tweet. We take the annotation as the ground truth. For each teenager, chronologically, we use the early 66% of his/her tweets as the training data, and the rest 34% as the testing data.

4.2   General Performance of Comment/Response Acts

Four different classifiers, including Naive Bayes, Logistic, SVM and Gaussian Process are used to perform the single-tweet based stress detection over the feature space of each stress category, respectively. Precision and recall are leveraged to evaluate the performance. With the comment/response acts selected within Δt after the tweet posted, assume for each stress category $C_i \in \mathcal{C}_{category}$, $TP(C_i, Lv_i, \Delta t), TN(C_i, Lv_i, \Delta t), FP(C_i, Lv_i, \Delta t), FN(C_i, Lv_i, \Delta t)$ represents the number of true positive, true negative, false positive and false negative samples detected of stress level Lv_i, respectively. Thus,

$$Precision(C_i, \Delta t) = \frac{1}{|\mathcal{L}_{evel}|} \sum_{Lv_j \in \mathcal{L}_{evel}} precision(C_i, Lv_j, \Delta t)$$

$$Recall(C_i, \Delta t) = \frac{1}{|\mathcal{L}_{evel}|} \sum_{Lv_j \in \mathcal{L}_{evel}} recall(C_i, Lv_j, \Delta t)$$

---

[1] One of the biggest Chinese micro-blog platform, http://t.qq.com/

where $precision(C_i, Lv_j, \Delta t) = \frac{TP(C_i, Lv_j, \Delta t)}{TP(C_i, Lv_j, \Delta t) + FP(C_i, Lv_i, \Delta t)}$, and $recall(C_i, Lv_j, \Delta t)$
$= \frac{TP(C_i, Lv_j, \Delta t)}{TP(C_i, Lv_j, \Delta t) + FN(C_i, Lv_j, \Delta t)}$.

Table 2. General Performance ($\Delta t = 30$ minutes)

Stress	Naive Bayes			Logistic			SVM			Gaussian		
	Prec.	Rec.	F-ms.	Prec.	Rec.	F-ms.	Prec.	Rec.	F-ms.	Prec.	Rec.	F-ms.
Aca	0.69	0.69	0.69	0.71	0.67	0.69	0.73	0.67	0.70	0.77	0.70	0.73
Aff	0.53	0.72	0.61	0.81	0.72	0.76	0.87	0.81	0.83	0.44	0.38	0.41
Inter	0.67	0.70	0.68	0.81	0.72	0.76	0.73	0.63	0.67	0.56	0.36	0.44
Self	0.60	0.66	0.53	0.69	0.67	0.68	0.66	0.64	0.65	0.32	0.33	0.33
Avg.	**0.62**	**0.69**	**0.65**	**0.76**	**0.70**	**0.72**	**0.75**	**0.69**	**0.71**	**0.52**	**0.44**	**0.48**

Table 2 compares the performance with $\Delta t = 30$ minutes. Averagely speaking, Logistic and SVM work the best in the four classifiers for all the stress categories, with the average F-measure over 70%, which is 10.7% better than NB, and 50% better than Gaussian.

4.3 Investigation of Time Sensitivity

We investigate the time sensitivity of comment/response acts with different Δt value. Logistic is selected as the classifier in this experiment since it performs the best of the three. Different time gap Δt ($= 10, 20, 30, 40,$ and $+\infty$ minutes) are selected to extract comment/response features, where all the interaction acts under a tweet are involved when $\Delta t = +\infty$. Fig. 1 shows the performance of different time sensitivity (Δt). Obviously, for each stress category, the detection results are time-sensitive. With the increase of Δt, the performance first improves and then falls again as Δt getting bigger. Particularly, when $\Delta t = 30min$, the detection performance reaches a peak, with the average F-measure over 70%. The result coincides with our daily observation. When a user posts a stressful tweet, his/her friends often comments in time to express care, comfort and encourage. With Δt increases within $[0, 30]$ (counted in minute), such effective information accumulates and makes the detection more accurate.

4.4 Impact of Comment/Response Acts

Table 3 compares the detection performance with/without comment/response acts under Logistic classifier. We set $\Delta t = 30$ minutes for time-sensitive interaction acts. Due to user's indirect expression, without interaction acts cannot provide enough information and performs worse. When involving the comment-/response acts, the average F-measure for all the stress categories reaches over 70%, outperforms the other case 23.5%, which proves the significance of time-sensitive comment/response acts in stress detection.

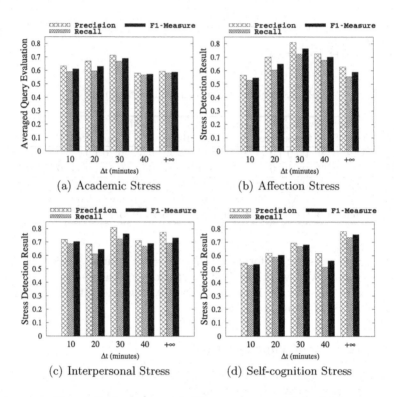

Fig. 1. Performance with different time sensitivity (Δt)

Table 3. Comparison with/without comment/response acts

Stress	Without C/R acts			With C/R acts		
	Prec.	Rec.	F-meas.	Prec.	Rec.	F-meas.
academic	0.596	0.553	0.574	0.713	0.669	0.690
affection	0.558	0.579	0.568	0.808	0.722	0.763
interpersonal	0.744	0.613	0.669	0.808	0.722	0.763
self-cognition	0.553	0.5	0.568	0.693	0.667	0.679
avg.	**0.613**	**0.561**	**0.586**	**0.756**	**0.695**	**0.724**

5   Conclusion

In this paper, together with content of tweets, we involve time-sensitive comment/response acts under a tweet to help better detect stress revealed from a teenager's tweet. Focusing on the four main categories of adolescent stress (academic, affection, interpersonal, and self-cognition), we specify content features for each stress category, and involve several novel features extracted from time-sensitive comment/response acts. 33 high school students aged 17 participated in our user study to evaluate the framework. Experimental results show that stress detection performance varies with different time sensitivity, and involving comment/response acts can better improve the F-measure of multi-category stress detection by 23.5%.

Acknowledgement. The work is supported by National Natural Science Foundation of China (61373022, 61370023, 61073004), and Chinese Major State Basic Research Development 973 Program (2011CB302203-2).

References

1. The week news. http://theweek.com/article/index/252199/the-rise-of-youth-suicide-in-china
2. Sohu news (2012). http://learning.sohu.com/s2012/shoot/
3. Sohu news (2013). http://learning.sohu.com/20130402/n371458123.shtml
4. USA today (2014). http://www.usatoday.com/story/news/nation/2014/02/11/stress-teens-psychological/5266739
5. Social media and the cost of caring (2015). http://www.pewinternet.org/files/2015/01/PI_Social-media-and-stress_0115151.pdf
6. Che, W., Li, Z., Guo, Y., Qin, B., Liu, T.: Multilingual dependency-based syntactic and semantic parsing. In: Proc. of CoNLL, pp. 49–54 (2009)
7. Che, W., Li, Z., Liu, T.: LTP: a chinese language technology platform. In: Proc. of Coling, pp. 13–16 (2010)
8. Choudhury, M., Counts, S., Horvitz, E.: Social media as a measurement tool of depression in populations. In: Proc. of ACM Web Science, pp. 47–56 (2013)
9. Choudhury, M., Gamon, M., Counts, S., Horvitz, E.: Prediction depression via social media. In: Proc. of ICWSM (2013)
10. Li, Q., Xue, Y., Jia, J., Feng, L.: Helping teenagers relieve psychological pressures: a micro-blog based system. In: Proc. of EDBT, pp. 660–663 (2014)
11. Lin, H., Jia, J., Guo, Q., Xue, Y., Huang, J., Cai, L., Feng, L.: Psychological stress detection from cross-media microblog data using deep sparse neural nework. In: Proc. of ICME, pp. 1–6 (2014)
12. Lin, H., Jia, J., Guo, Q., Xue, Y., Li, Q., Huang, J., Cai, L., Feng, L.: User-level psychological stress detection from social media using deep neural network. In: Proc. of MM, pp. 507–516 (2014)
13. Park, M., McDonald, D., Cha, M.: Perception differences between the depressed and non-depressed users in twitter. In: Proc. of ICWSM (2013)
14. Tan, C., Lee, L., Tang, J., Jiang, L., Zhou, M., Li, P.: User-level sentiment analysis incorporating social networks. In: Proc. of SIGKDD, pp. 1397–1405 (2011)
15. Wang, X., Zhang, C., Ji, Y., Sun, L., Wu, L.: A depression detection model based on sentiment analysis in micro-blog social network. In: Proc. of PAKDD (2013)
16. Xue, Y., Li, Q., Jin, L., Feng, L., Clifton, D.A., Clifford, G.D.: Detecting adolescent psychological pressures from micro-blog. In: Zhang, Y., Yao, G., He, J., Wang, L., Smalheiser, N.R., Yin, X. (eds.) HIS 2014. LNCS, vol. 8423, pp. 83–94. Springer, Heidelberg (2014)
17. Yang, Y., Jia, J., Zhang, S., Wu, B., Chen, Q., Li, J., Xing, C., Tang, J.: How do your friends on social media disclose your emotions. In: Proc. of AAAI

18. Shen, Y., Kuo, T., Yeh, I., Chen, T., Lin, S.: Exploiting temporal information in a two-stage classification framework for content-based depression detection. In: Proc. of PAKDD, pp. 276–288 (2013)
19. Zhang, Y., Tang, J., Sun, J., Chen, Y., Rao, J.: Moodcast: emotion prediction via dynamic continuous factor graph model. In: Proc. of ICDM
20. Zhao, J., Dong, L., Wu, J., Xu, K.: Moodlens: an emoticon-based sentiment analysis system for chinese tweets. In: Proc. of SIGKDD, pp. 1528–1531 (2012)

Artificial Intelligence for Knowledge Management

A Novel Approach for Resolving Knowledge Inconsistency on Ontology Syntactic Level

Trung Van Nguyen[1], Jason J. Jung[2], and Hanh Huu Hoang[3]([✉])

[1] College of Sciences, Hue University, 77 Nguyen Hue Street, Hue, Vietnam
nvtrung@hueuni.edu.vn
[2] Department of Computer Engineering,
Chung-Ang University, Seoul 156-756, Republic of Korea
j2jung@gmail.com
[3] Hue University, 3 Le Loi Street, Hue, Vietnam
hhhanh@hueuni.edu.vn

Abstract. Solving the inconsistency of knowledge is a challenging task in the ontology integration. There are two levels for processing knowledge inconsistence which are based on logics: syntactic level and semantic level. In this paper, we propose a consensus-based method to resolve inconsistent knowledge on the syntactic level, where a knowledge state can be represented by a conjunction of literals.

Keywords: Ontology integration · Consensus theory · Syntactic level · Conjunction · Inconsistency

1 Introduction

The inconsistency consists of two levels in knowledge processing based on logics [4]: the syntactic level and the semantic level. In the syntactic level, knowledge states can be represented by logic expressions, and they are in conflict if expressions' syntaxes are different. Meanwhile, in the semantic level, the knowlege inconsistency and consistency are considered further at their interpretations [7].

In this paper, we propose a consensus-based method to resolve the knowledge inconsistency on its syntactic level. One of the most important things in consensus-based methods is the distance function of two elements in the universe set. There have been several and similar approaches to evaluate distance between two logic expressions: Zhisheng Huang, Frank van Harmelen [3] measure a so-called relevance between two formulas by considering the number of their common and different symbols. Ferilli [1,2] further considered occurrences of objects, predicates in the formulas based on taxonomic background knowledge such as WordNet ontology. We assume that, a knowledge state can be expressed as a *conjunction of literals* as [4]. However, by using other *distance function of two sets of symbols* than [4], we analyse and prove some interesting properties of postulates for consensus functions. Based on these properties, we propose a new algorithm for determining the consensus for a conflict profile of conjunctions.

© IFIP International Federation for Information Processing 2015
T. Dillon (Ed.): IFIP AI 2015, IFIP AICT 465, pp. 39–49, 2015.
DOI: 10.1007/978-3-319-25261-2_4

Our paper will be detailed and structured as follows: Section 2 formalises the problem of determining the consensus for a conflict profile of conjunctions. Meanwhile, Section 3 presents postulates for the consensus function and analyse their properties. Based on this, we propose a new algorithm for determining the consensus in Section 4. The paper is then concluded with discussions and future work in Section 5.

2   Problems of Determining Consensus for a Conflict Profile of Conjunctions

In this section, we recall essential notions directly used in formalising the problem of determining the consensus for a conflict profile of conjunctions in Nguyen's work [4].

Assume that, for expressing opinion about a subject in the real world, an expert agent uses a conjunction of literals $t_1 \wedge t_2 \wedge \ldots t_k$, where $t_i \in \mathbf{L}$ or $t_i = \neg t'_{i'}$ and $t'_{i'} \in \mathbf{L}$. $\mathbf{L}$ is a definite set of symbols, which expresses a positive logic value, reference to an event in the real world.

A conjunction x can be expressed as (x^+, x^-), where x^+ contains $t \in \mathbf{L}$, and x^- contains t and $\neg t \in \mathbf{L}$. For example, $x = a \wedge \neg b \wedge c$, which $a, b, c \in \mathbf{L}$ can be written as (x^+, x^-), where $x^+ = \{a, c\}$ and $x^- = \{b\}$.

By $Conj(\mathbf{L})$ we denote the set of all conjunctions with symbols from set $\mathbf{L}$.

Definition 1 (Nonconflicting conjunction). *A conjunction (x^+, x^-) where $x^+, x^- \subseteq \mathbf{L}$ is nonconflicting if $x^+ \cap x^- = \emptyset$.*

Definition 2 (Inconsistent conjunctions, sharply inconsistent conjunctions). *Let $x = (x^+, x^-), x' = (x'^+, x'^-) \in Conj(\mathbf{L})$ are nonconflicting conjunctions. We say:*

(a) x is inconsistent with x' if

$$x^+ \cap x'^- \neq \emptyset \quad or \quad x'^+ \cap x^- \neq \emptyset \ ,$$

(b) x is sharply inconsistent with x' if they are inconsistent and

$$x^+ \cap x'^+ = \emptyset \quad and \quad x^- \cap x'^- = \emptyset \ .$$

Definition 3. *A set of nonconflicting conjunctions*

$$\mathbf{X} = \left\{ x_i = (x^+, x^-) \in Conj(\mathbf{L}) : i = 1, 2, \ldots, n \right\}$$

is inconsistent if $\bigcup_{x \in \mathbf{X}} x^+ \cap \bigcup_{x \in \mathbf{X}} x^- \neq \emptyset$, otherwise it is consistent.

Then we propose an our own distance function $d_\wedge$ for conjunctions. This function is based on the distance between sets of symbols.

Definition 4 (Distance between two finite sets). *By the distance between two finite sets* $\mathbf{X}_1$, $\mathbf{X}_2$ *we understand the following number*

$$\eta(\mathbf{X}_1, \mathbf{X}_2) = \frac{card(\mathbf{X}_1 \triangle \mathbf{X}_2)}{card(\mathbf{L})} \tag{1}$$

where, $card(\mathbf{L})$ *is the number of elements in* $\mathbf{L}$, *and* $\mathbf{X}_1 \triangle \mathbf{X}_2$ *is symmetric difference of the two sets* $\mathbf{X}_1$ *and* $\mathbf{X}_2$.

Definition 5 (Distance between two conjunctions [4]). *By the distance between two conjunctions* $x_1, x_2 \in Conj(\mathbf{L})$ *we understand the following number*

$$d_\wedge(x_1, x_2) = w_1.\eta(x_1^+, x_2^+) + w_2.\eta(x_1^-, x_2^-) \ ,$$

where

- $\eta(x_1^+, x_2^+)$ *is the distance between sets of nonnegated symbols in conjunctions* x_1 *and* x_2.
- $\eta(x_1^-, x_2^-)$ *is the distance between sets of negated symbols in conjunctions* x_1 *and* x_2.
- w_1, w_2 *are the weights of distances* $\eta(x_1^+, x_2^+)$ *and* $\eta(x_1^-, x_2^-)$ *in distance* $d_\wedge(x_1, x_2)$, *respectively, which satisfy the conditions:*

$$w_1 + w_2 = 1 \ \ and \ \ 0 < w_1, w_2 < 1 \ .$$

In this paper, we use $w_1 = w_2 = \frac{1}{2}$.

By $\mathbf{U}$ we denote a finite set of objects representing possible values for a knowledge state. We also denote:

- $\prod_k(\mathbf{U})$ is the set of all k-element subsets (with repetitions) of set $\mathbf{U}$ ($k \in \mathbb{N}$, set of natural numbers).
- $\prod(\mathbf{U}) = \bigcup_{k \in \mathbb{N}} \prod_k(\mathbf{U})$ is the set of all nonempty subsets with repetitions of set $\mathbf{U}$. An element in $\prod(\mathbf{U})$ is called as a conflict profile.

The problem of determining consensus for a conflict profile of conjunctions is formulated as follows [4]:

For a given conflict profile of conjunctions

$$\mathsf{X} := \{x_i = (x_i^+, x_i^-) \in Conj(\mathbf{L}) : i = 1, 2, \ldots, n\}.$$

It is necessary to determine a conjunction $x^* \in Conj(\mathbf{L})$, *called as a consensus of* X.

3   Consensus Functions and Postulates for Consensus

We also start with recalling definitions in [4]:

Definition 6 (Consensus function for profiles). *By a consensus function for profiles of conjunctions we understand a function*

$$C : \prod(Conj(\mathbf{L})) \to 2^{Conj(\mathbf{L})} \ ,$$

which satisfies one or more of the following postulates.

P1. For each conjunction $(x^{*^+}, x^{*^-}) \in C(\mathsf{X})$ there should be $\bigcap\limits_{x \in \mathsf{X}} x^+ \subseteq x^{*^+}$ and

$\bigcap\limits_{x \in \mathsf{X}} x^- \subseteq x^{*^-}$.

P2. For each conjunction $(x^{*^+}, x^{*^-}) \in C(\mathsf{X})$ there should be $x^{*^+} \subseteq \bigcup\limits_{x \in \mathsf{X}} x^+$ and

$x^{*^-} \subseteq \bigcup\limits_{x \in \mathsf{X}} x^-$.

P3. If X is consistent then conjunction $(\bigcup\limits_{x \in \mathsf{X}} x^+, \bigcup\limits_{x \in \mathsf{X}} x^-)$ should be a consensus

of X.

P4. For each conjunction $(x^{*^+}, x^{*^-}) \in C(\mathsf{X})$, there should be $x^{*^+} \cap x^{*^-} = \emptyset$.

P5. A consensus $x^* \in C(\mathsf{X})$ should minimize the sum of distances:

$$\sum\limits_{x \in \mathsf{X}} d_{\wedge}(x^*, x) = min \left\{ \sum\limits_{x \in \mathsf{X}} d_{\wedge}(x', x) \mid x' \in Conj(\mathbf{L}) \right\}$$

P6. For each symbol $z \in \mathbf{L}$ and a consensus $x^* \in C(\mathsf{X})$, the form of appearance of z in x^* depends only on its forms of appearance in conjunctions belonging to X.

In a consensus $(x^{*^+}, x^{*^-}) \in C(\mathsf{X})$, set x^{*^+} (resp., set x^{*^-}) is called as the positive component *(resp., the negative component).*

By C_{co} we denote the set of all consensus functions for profile of conjunctions. Then, we analyse properties of the postulates for consensus functions. We denote:

- A consensus function C satisfies a postulate P for *a profile* X written as $C(\mathsf{X}) \vdash P$.
- A consensus function C satisfies a postulate P for *all profiles* , written as $C \vdash P$.
- A postulate P is satisfied for all *consensus functions* $C \in C_{co}$, written as $C_{co} \vdash P$.

The first proposed theorem presented below shows that postulates P1 and P2 are the consequences of postulate P5.

Theorem 1. *A consensus function $C \in C_{co}$ which satisfies postulate P5 should also satisfies postulates P1 and P2; that is $(C \vdash P5) \Rightarrow (C \vdash P1 \wedge C \vdash P2)$.*

Proof. We prove (a) $(C \vdash P5) \Rightarrow (C \vdash P1)$ and (b) $(C \vdash P5) \Rightarrow (C \vdash P2)$ as follow:

(a) $C \vdash P5 \Rightarrow C \vdash P1$

Let $\mathsf{X} \in \prod(Conj(\mathbf{L}))$ *is a profile of conjunctions, $C \in C_{co}$ is a consensus function which satisfies postulate P5. Let $(x^{*+}, x^{*-}) \in C(\mathsf{X})$ is a consensus of X. To prove P1 is also satisfied by C, we have to prove*

$$\bigcap_{x \in \mathsf{X}} x^+ \subseteq x^{*+} \tag{2}$$

and

$$\bigcap_{x \in \mathsf{X}} x^- \subseteq x^{*-} \tag{3}$$

For the first dependence, let's assume that $\bigcap_{x \in \mathsf{X}} x^+ \nsubseteq x^{*+}$; this means, there exists a symbol $t \in \bigcap_{x \in \mathsf{X}} x^+$ such that $t \notin x^{*+}$. In this case we create set $x'^* = (x'^{*+}, x^{*-})$ where $x'^{*+} = x^{*+} \cup \{t\}$.
For each $x \in \mathsf{X}$, we have

$$\eta(x'^{*+}, x^+) = \frac{card(x'^{*+} \bigtriangleup x^+)}{card(\mathbf{L})}$$
$$= \frac{card((x^{*+} \cup \{t\}) \bigtriangleup x^+)}{card(\mathbf{L})} .$$

Because of $t \notin x^{*+}$ and $t \in \bigcap_{x \in \mathsf{X}} x^+$, we have $\forall x \in \mathsf{X}$:

$$card((x^{*+} \cup \{t\}) \bigtriangleup x^+) = card(x^{*+} \bigtriangleup x^+) - 1$$

So, we have $\forall x \in \mathsf{X}$:

$$\eta(x'^{*+}, x^+) = \frac{card((x^{*+} \cup \{t\}) \div x^+)}{card(\mathbf{L})}$$
$$= \frac{card(x^{*+} \bigtriangleup x^+) - 1}{card(\mathbf{L})}$$
$$< \frac{card(x^{*+} \bigtriangleup x^+)}{card(\mathbf{L})} = \eta(x^{*+}, x^+) .$$

Finally, we have:

$$\sum_{x \in \mathsf{X}} \eta(x'^{*+}, x^+) < \sum_{x \in \mathsf{X}} \eta(x^{*+}, x^+)$$

$$d_\wedge(x'^*, \mathsf{X}) = \sum_{x \in \mathsf{X}} \left(\frac{1}{2} \cdot \eta(x'^{*+}, x^+) + \frac{1}{2} \cdot \eta(x^{*-}, x^-) \right)$$

$$< \sum_{x \in \mathsf{X}} \left(\frac{1}{2} \cdot \eta(x^{*+}, x^+) + \frac{1}{2} \cdot \eta(x^{*-}, x^-) \right)$$

$$= d_\wedge(x^*, \mathsf{X})$$

This is contradictory to the assumption that $\left(((x^{*+}, x^{*-}) \in C(\mathsf{X}) \wedge (C(\mathsf{X}) \vdash P5) \right)$. So, we have (2) is satisfied. The (3) can be proved similarly.

(b) P5 ⊢ P2 can be easily and similarly proved as the proof of P5 ⊢ P1. We omit the proof due to the limit of pages.

Another property of the postulate P5 is also stated in [4], wherein definition of distance between sets, and therefor conjunctions are defined slightly different to ours in this paper, as:

Theorem 2. *The positive and negative components of a consensus satisfying postulate P5 can be determined in an independent way; that is, conjunction (x^{*+}, x^{*-}) is a consensus of X if and only if conjunction $(x^{*+}, \emptyset)$ is a consensus of profile $\mathsf{X}' = \{(x_i^+, \emptyset) : i = 1, 2, \ldots, n\}$, and conjunction $(\emptyset, x^{*-})$ is a consensus of profile $\mathsf{X}'' = \{(\emptyset, x_i^-) : i = 1, 2, \ldots, n\}$ [4].*

Theorem 2 is still valid in our paper's context. However, this theorem does not show how to construct a consensus of a conflict profile. Actually, the consensus can be determined based on the following theorem.

Theorem 3. *Let $\mathsf{X} = \{x_i, i = 1, 2, \ldots, n\}$ is a profile of conjunctions, $\mathsf{X} \in \prod(Conj(\mathbf{L}))$. We denote*

- $\mathbf{Z}^+ = \bigcup_{x \in \mathsf{X}} x^+.$
- $\mathbf{Z}^- = \bigcup_{x \in \mathsf{X}} x^-.$
- $f^+(z) = card\{x_i \in \mathsf{X} \mid x_i^+ \ni z\}.$
- $f^-(z) = card\{x_i \in \mathsf{X} \mid x_i^- \ni z\}.$

Assume that $C(X)$ satisfies postulate P5. In this case, $x^* = (x^{*+}, x^{*-})$ is a consensus of X if and only if (a) $x^{*+} = \left\{ z \in \mathbf{Z}^+ \mid f^+(z) >= \frac{n}{2} \right\}$ and (b) $x^{-+} = \left\{ z \in \mathbf{Z}^- \mid f^-(z) >= \frac{n}{2} \right\}$.

Proof. As Theorem 2, we can formulate a consensus $x^* = (x^{*+}, x^{*-})$ satisfying postulate P5 by independently formulating x^{*+} and x^{*-} for $\mathsf{X}^+ = \{x_i^+, i = 1, 2, \ldots, n\}$ and $\mathsf{X}^- = \{x_i^-, i = 1, 2, \ldots, n\}$. We have to prove that (a) $x^{*+} = \left\{ z \in \mathbf{Z}^+ \mid f^+(z) >= \frac{n}{2} \right\}$. The proof for (b) is similar.

First, as Theorem 1, x^{*+} contains only literals belonging to $\mathbf{Z}^+$. We will prove that, for any conjunction $x \in Conj(\mathbf{L})$, we have:

(i) If $z \in Z^+$ such that $f^+(z) \geq \dfrac{n}{2}$ and $z \notin x^+$ then $d_\wedge((x^+, x^-), \mathsf{X}^+) \leq d_\wedge((x^+ \cup \{z\}, x^-), \mathsf{X}^+)$, and

(ii) If $z \in Z^+$ such that $f^+(z) < \dfrac{n}{2}$ and $z \notin x^+$ then $d_\wedge((x^+, x^-), \mathsf{X}^+) > d_\wedge((x^+ \cup \{z\}, x^-), \mathsf{X}^+)$.

We have:

$$d_\wedge((x^+ \cup \{z\}, x^-), \mathsf{X}) = \sum_{y \in \mathsf{X}} \left(\frac{1}{2} \cdot \frac{card((x^+ \cup \{z\}) \bigtriangleup y^+)}{card(\mathbf{L})} + \frac{1}{2} \cdot \frac{card(x^- \bigtriangleup y^-)}{card(\mathbf{L})} \right)$$

and

$$\frac{card((x^+ \cup \{z\}) \bigtriangleup y^+)}{card(\mathbf{L})} = \begin{cases} \dfrac{card(x^+ \bigtriangleup y^+) - 1}{card(\mathbf{L})} & \text{if } y^+ \ni z, \\[3mm] \dfrac{card(x^+ \bigtriangleup y^+) + 1}{card(\mathbf{L})} & \text{if } y^+ \not\ni z. \end{cases}$$

Let $\mathsf{X}_{\overline{z}} := \{x \in \mathsf{X} \mid x^+ \ni z\}$ and $\mathsf{X}_{\overline{z}} := \{x \in \mathsf{X} \mid x^+ \not\ni z\}$. We have, $card(\mathsf{X}_z) = f^+(z)$ and $card(\mathsf{X}_{\overline{z}}) = n - f^+(z)$. So:

$$\sum_{y \in \mathsf{X}} \frac{card((x^+ \cup \{z\}) \bigtriangleup y^+)}{card(\mathbf{L})} = \sum_{y \in \mathsf{X}_z} \frac{card((x^+ \cup \{z\}) \bigtriangleup y^+)}{card(\mathbf{L})} + \sum_{y \in \mathsf{X}_{\overline{z}}} \frac{card((x^+ \cup \{z\}) \bigtriangleup y^+)}{card(\mathbf{L})}$$

$$= \sum_{y \in \mathsf{X}_z} \frac{card(x^+ \bigtriangleup y^+) - 1}{card(\mathbf{L})} + \sum_{y \in \mathsf{X}_{\overline{z}}} \frac{card(x^+ \bigtriangleup y^+) + 1}{card(\mathbf{L})}$$

$$= \sum_{y \in \mathsf{X}} \frac{card(x^+ \bigtriangleup y^+)}{card(\mathbf{L})} + \frac{-f^+(z) + n - f^+(z)}{card(\mathbf{L})}$$

$$= \sum_{y \in \mathsf{X}} \frac{card(x^+ \bigtriangleup y^+)}{card(\mathbf{L})} + \frac{n - 2.f^+(z)}{card(\mathbf{L})} .$$

Finally, we have

$$d_\wedge((x^+ \cup \{z\}, x^-), \mathsf{X}) = \sum_{y \in \mathsf{X}} \left(\frac{1}{2} \cdot \frac{card((x^+ \cup \{z\}) \bigtriangleup y^+)}{card(\mathbf{L})} + \frac{1}{2} \cdot \frac{card(x^- \bigtriangleup y^-)}{card(\mathbf{L})} \right)$$

$$= \sum_{y \in \mathsf{X}} \left(\frac{1}{2} \cdot \left(\frac{card(x^+ \bigtriangleup y^+)}{card(\mathbf{L})} + \frac{n - 2.f^+(z)}{card(\mathbf{L})} \right) + \frac{1}{2} \cdot \frac{card(x^- \bigtriangleup y^-)}{card(\mathbf{L})} \right)$$

$$= d_\wedge(x, \mathsf{X}) + \frac{1}{2} \cdot \frac{n - 2.f^+(z)}{card(\mathbf{L})}$$

Therefore, when $n - 2.f^+(z) \leq 0$, or $f^+(z) \leq \dfrac{n}{2}$, adding z to x^+ will not make increase sum of distances of x to X. Otherwise, when $f^+(z) < \dfrac{n}{2}$, adding z to x^+ will make increase sum of distances of x to X. Finally, (i) and (ii) are satisfied.

Back to proving (a), we can see that, start at the set $\left\{ z \in \mathbf{Z}^+ \mid f^+(z) >= \dfrac{n}{2} \right\}$, we can not remove any element(s) from this set, and can not add any other element(s) from $\mathbf{Z}^+$ in process of determining the positive component of the consensus. Hence, this is the optimal positive component of consensus! ((a) is satisfied).

4 Proposed Algorithm for Determining Consensus

4.1 Algorithm

Based on our proposed theorems in the previous section, we introduce an algorithm for determining the consensus $x^* = (x^{*+}, x^{*-})$ for profile $X \in \prod(Conj(\mathbf{L}))$ as **Algorithm 1**.

Input: Profile $X \in \prod(Conj(\mathbf{L}))$, $X = \{(x_i^+, x_i^-), i = 1, 2, \ldots, n\}$,
   $x_i^+ \cap x_i^- = \emptyset$ $\forall i = 1, 2, \ldots, n$.
Output: Consensus $x^* \in Conj(\mathbf{L})$ satisfies one or more postulates in {P4, P1, P2, P3, P5}.

begin

   $\mathbf{Z}^+ := \bigcup_{x \in X} x^+; \quad \mathbf{Z}^- := \bigcup_{x \in X} x^-;$

   foreach $z \in \mathbf{Z}^+$ **do**
      $f^+(z) := card\{x \in X \mid x^+ \ni z\};$

   foreach $z \in \mathbf{Z}^-$ **do**
      $f^-(z) := card\{x \in X \mid x^- \ni z\};$

(a) $x^{*+} := \{z \in \mathbf{Z}^+ \mid f^+(z) \geq \frac{n}{2}\};$

   $x^{*-} := \{z \in \mathbf{Z}^- \mid f^-(z) \geq \frac{n}{2}\};$

   if $(x^{*+} \cup x^{*-} \neq \emptyset)$ **then**

(b)   **foreach** $z \in x^{*+} \cap x^{*-}$ **do**
         if $d_\wedge((x^{*+} \setminus \{z\}, x^{*-}), X) < d_\wedge((x^{*+}, x^{*-} \setminus \{z\}), X)$ **then**
            $x^{*+} := x^{*+} \setminus \{z\};$
         else
            $x^{*-} := x^{*-} \setminus \{z\};$

   else
      if $(\mathbf{Z}^+ \cap \mathbf{Z}^- = \emptyset)$ **then**
(c) $x^* := (\mathbf{Z}^+, \mathbf{Z}^-);$
      else
(d) $x^* := x_1;$
         for $i := 2$ **to** n **do**
            if $d_\wedge(x^*, X) > d_\wedge(x, X)$ **then**
               $x^* := x_i$

Algorithm 1. Determine consensus for profile of conjunctions

As shown in **Algorithm 1**, we start by finding the consensus satisfying postulate P5 (step (a)). After that:

(i) If both positive and negative of the P5-consensus are empty, the algorithm will find the consensus satisfying postulate P3 (step (c)) if X is consistent. In case of X is inconsistent, as step (d), the algorithm will choose from X an element which has minimum sum of distances to others elements in X. The consensus in this case satisfies postulate P4 (because $x_i^+ \cap x_i^- = \emptyset$, $\forall i = 1, 2, \ldots, n$).

(ii) If in step (a), the positive or negative component is not empty, we refine them for satisfying postulate P4, and also ensure that the sum of distances to elements in X is minimal.

Beside that, in all cases of the two above branches (i) and (ii), we construct x^{*+} (respectively x^{*-}) from $\mathbf{Z}^+$ (respectively $\mathbf{Z}^-$). Therefore, the consensus always satisfies postulate P2. The consensus also satisfies postulate P1 because it construct from consensus which satisfies postulate P5, after that, elements which are removed because of their occurrences are smaller than $\frac{n}{2}$.

The computational complexity of **Algorithm 1** is $O(n.m^2)$, where n is the number of elements in X, $m = max\left\{ card(\bigcup_{x \in X} x^+), card(\bigcup_{x \in X} x^-) \right\}$.

4.2   Example

Let's assume that, to specify the property *hasSpouse* in an ontology, an agent can use a conjunction in $Conj(\mathbf{L})$ where $\mathbf{L} = \{t_1, t_2, t_3, t_4\}$. These symbols represent the following facts:

- t_1: *hasSpouse* is symmetric.
- t_2: *hasSpouse* is reflexive.
- t_3: *hasSpouse* is functional.
- t_4: *hasSpouse* is a subproperty of *hasRelationshipWith*.

6 agents $a_1, a_2, \ldots, a_6$ express their opinions as **Table 1**:

Table 1. Knowledge states for example

Agent	Knowledge state
a_1	$t_1 \wedge \neg t_2 \wedge t_3 \wedge t_4$
a_2	$t_1 \wedge \neg t_3 \wedge \neg t_4$
a_3	$t_1 \wedge \neg t_3$
a_4	$t_1 \wedge \neg t_3 \wedge \neg t_4$
a_5	$\neg t_1 \wedge t_3 \wedge \neg t_4$
a_6	t_3

We will use **Algorithm 1** to determine consensus from opinions of the above 6 agents. Firstly, we formalize the profile X:

$$\mathsf{X} = \left\{ (\{t_1, t_3, t_4\}, \{t_2\}), 2 * (\{t_1\}, \{t_3, t_4\}), (\{t_1\}, \{t_3\}), (\{t_3\}, \{t_1\}), (\{t_3\}, \emptyset) \right\} .$$

After step (a) of the algorithm, we have $x^{*+} = \{t_1, t_3\}$ and $x^{*-} = \{t_3, t_4\}$.

Because $x^{*+} \cup x^{*-} \neq \emptyset$, we have to find a way to remove common literal(s) of the two components (as step (b)): With $x^{*+} \cap x^{*-} = \{t_3\}$, we compare two sums of distances $d_\wedge((\{t_1\}, \{t_3, t_4\}), \mathsf{X})$ and $d_\wedge((\{t_1, t_3\}, \{t_4\}), \mathsf{X})$. We easily have

- $d_\wedge((\{t_1\}, \{t_3, t_4\}), \mathsf{X}) = \dfrac{15}{8}$,
- $d_\wedge((\{t_1, t_3\}, \{t_4\}), \mathsf{X}) = \dfrac{13}{8}$.

Hence, consensus of X is $(\{t_1, t_3\}, \{t_4\})$, or $t_1 \wedge t_3 \wedge \neg t_4$.

5   Conclusion

In this paper, we formalised a method to determine the consensus of knowledge states presented as conjunctions of literals. We defined a distance between two conjunctions, proved relevant theorems for dependencies of postulates. Based on these theorems, we proposed a novel algorithm for determining the consensus for a profile of conjunctions.

As future work, we would like to analyse opportunities of using the more complex structure for presenting knowledge state than the conjunction or disjunction of literals. We also would like to apply the **Algorithm 1** to determining consensus axioms in process of the ontological engineering in a wiki-based environment [5,6] such as collaborative ontology development or ontological annotation.

Acknowledgement. This work was partly supported by the National Research Foundation of Korea (NRF) grant funded by the Korea government (MSIP) (NRF-2014R1A2A2A05007154).

References

1. Ferilli, S., Biba, M., Di Mauro, N., Basile, T.M.A., Esposito, F.: Plugging taxonomic similarity in first-order logic horn clauses comparison. In: Serra, R., Cucchiara, R. (eds.) AI*IA 2009. LNCS, vol. 5883, pp. 131–140. Springer, Heidelberg (2009)
2. Ferilli, S., Basile, T.M.A., Di Mauro, N., Biba, M., Esposito, F.: Similarity-guided clause generalization. In: Basili, R., Pazienza, M.T. (eds.) AI*IA 2007. LNCS (LNAI), vol. 4733, pp. 278–289. Springer, Heidelberg (2007)
3. Huang, Z., van Harmelen, F.: Using semantic distances for reasoning with inconsistent ontologies. In: Sheth, A.P., Staab, S., Dean, M., Paolucci, M., Maynard, D., Finin, T., Thirunarayan, K. (eds.) ISWC 2008. LNCS, vol. 5318, pp. 178–194. Springer, Heidelberg (2008)

4. Nguyen, N.T.: Advanced Methods for Inconsistent Knowledge Management (Advanced Information and Knowledge Processing). Springer (2007). http://dx.doi.org/10.1007/978-1-84628-889-0
5. Tudorache, T., Noy, N.F., Tu, S., Musen, M.A.: Supporting collaborative ontology development in Protégé. In: Sheth, A.P., Staab, S., Dean, M., Paolucci, M., Maynard, D., Finin, T., Thirunarayan, K. (eds.) ISWC 2008. LNCS, vol. 5318, pp. 17–32. Springer, Heidelberg (2008). http://www.springerlink.com/index/uu1453660t047775.pdf
6. Tudorache, T., Nyulas, C., Noy, N.F., Musen, M.A.: WebProtege: A collaborative ontology editor and knowledge acquisition tool for the web. Semantic Web **4**(1), 89–99 (2013)
7. Van Nguyen, T., Hoang, H.H.: A consensus-based method for solving concept-level conflict in ontology integration. In: Hwang, D., Jung, J.J., Nguyen, N.-T. (eds.) ICCCI 2014. LNCS, vol. 8733, pp. 414–423. Springer, Heidelberg (2014)

Dynamic Data Mart for Business Intelligence

E. Chang[1(✉)], W. Rahayu[2], M. Diallo[3], and M. Machizaud[3]

[1] The University of New South Wales, Sydney, NSW, Australia
Elizabeth.chang@unsw.edu.au
[2] La Trobe University, Bundoora, Melbourne, VIC, Australia
W.Rahayu@latrobe.edu.au
[3] Ecole Nationale Supérieure des Mines d'Albi, Albi, France
{mariam.diallo,matthieu.machizaud}@mines-albi.fr

Abstract. Companies today have several major issues while managing information. Many subsidiaries and departments have developed their own Data Management which has led to a multitude of Operational Databases and sometimes a multitude of Data Marts, policies and processes. Thus, these systems lack sustainability because they are not dynamic and not self-organizing, and so they do not adapt to the continuous needs arising from evolution that the companies experience. The Dynamic Data Mart architecture is built around 6 main functions, namely the 3Ms (Data Mining, Data Marshalling and Data Meshing) and the 3Rs (Recommendation, Reconciliation and Representation), which will address the aforementioned problems. Once the totality of the data have been loaded into a single Data Warehouse, the Dynamics Data Marts address these problems by mining the user's behavior and the user's decision making processes and continuously and automatically adapting the Data Mart to the needs of the users. Dynamic Data Marts create adapted dimensions, facts, data associations and views and then automatically find the ones that are not used anymore. These latter are then automatically dropped by the system, or can be presented to the IT manager if needed for validation of their removal.

Keywords: Dynamic data mart · Data integration · Disparate data sources

1 Introduction

Current Enterprise Data Warehouses are systems which have been constructed by experts in order to provide answers in the best way possible to business oriented questions. These questions have been posed by middle and top end managers, who needed to answer these questions contemporaneously to the building of the Data Warehouse. But an important problem remains: companies and organizations are in constant evolution in order to adapt to the market and to the changing environment. Processes, therefore, have to change and in this context, Data Warehouses still remain the same and often fail to meet the expectation of business users. Changing them could be arduous, time consuming and have a very long time duration. At the same time, business users have an increasing need to access a large amount of Data very quickly in

© IFIP International Federation for Information Processing 2015
T. Dillon (Ed.): IFIP AI 2015, IFIP AICT 465, pp. 50–63, 2015.
DOI: 10.1007/978-3-319-25261-2_5

order to make better decisions. This has led different subsidiaries and departments to develop their own information systems, and therefore a large number of Data Bases and Data Marts exists within organizations (Figure 1). Therefore, as the demand of accurate, organized and useful data is increasing, an effective Data Management system is needed, in order to have consistency within the company and allow every level of manager to have access to consistent and reliable data.

2   Key Issues

Three key issues have been identified in current Data Warehouse management systems namely :

1. A multiplicity of Data Marts exist in many big companies and organizations

The information is spread among a number of subsidiaries and departments. Each subsidiary and department has developed its own system in order to store and access the data. Each of them may have created their own Data Warehouses and Data marts, in order to provide answers to very specific questions, resulting in a multiplicity of procedures, policies and user interfaces to manage the same Business processes. This often leads to inconsistency which becomes a real problem when the organization needs to have a larger overview of the information and when they need to drill down into and roll up over the different subsidiaries and departments.

2. Existing Data Warehouses are not sustainable

After a few years of use, as it is frequently not possible to answer new business question, because of lack of malleability of these Data Warehouses. The structure of the Data Warehouse and of Data Mart needs to be changed by the Data Warehouse Manager in order to answer these new questions, and it can take a lot of time to see these changes done. This important lead time results in the inefficient use of the total amount of data that the company has, resulting in the diminution of the creativity and of the curiosity of executives, and in the high possibility of missing important information due to a lack of freedom in the access to data. Data Marts are therefore not sustainable because they do not adapt easily to the changes of business processes and of policies.

3. Existing Data Warehouses cannot be dynamic or self-organize

This lack of sustainability of the data mart leads to the necessity of managing them constantly, in order to have a Data mart which is continuously consistent with the Business Processes. This process is particularly time-consuming and needs continuous care of the system: the quantity of data is indeed always growing whereas the processes are always evolving inside of the company. Therefore, the Data Warehouse is a hindrance to the development of the company, because it is not as dynamic and self-organized as they should be in order to answer the constantly changing needs of its users.

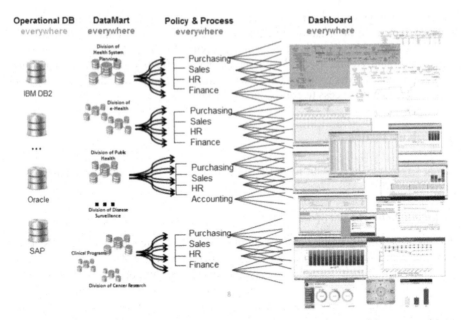

Fig. 1. Traditional corporate Big Data Management and Database, Data Mart everywhere, leading to multiple overlapping policies, processes and Dashboards everywhere.

3   Existing Corporate Data Warehouse Implementation Architectures

Based on the latest Gartner (2015) study, the Corporate Data Warehouse data management architectures can be divided into the following 4 categories:

Traditional Data Warehouse: manages historical data coming from various structured sources. Data is mainly loaded through bulk and batch loading. It requires high capabilities for system availability, and administration and management, given the mixed workload capabilities for queries and user skills breakdown. This is a materialized or physical data warehouse.

Operational Data Warehouse: manages structured data that is loaded continuously in support of embedded analytics in applications, real-time data warehouses and operational data stores. Primarily supports reporting and automated queries, to support operational needs. This is a materialized or physical data warehouse/ repository.

Logical Data Warehouse: manages data variety and volume for both structured and other content data types such as machine data, text documents, images and videos. Supports queries using data from sources other than the data warehouse DBMS alone. This combines materialized repository (for structured data) and non-materialised data warehouse where an enterprise integrated meta-model is defined that handles the access to the individual data repository. The main components of this DW are the meta-data, a data virtualization layer that can process data in their original source, and a distributed processing system. This is the most current architecture/methodology especially to support big data variety of data sets.

Context Independent Data Warehouse: has the capability to establish ``schema on read" approaches for new and even existing data values, variants of data form and new relationships. Also supports search, graph and other advanced capabilities for discovering new information models. There are no specific performance requirements and this option is favoured by advanced users such as data scientists or data miners, resulting in freeform queries across multiple data types.

Conventional data warehouses designs, which are primarily centered on relational databases have their own limitations. The two well-known models/schemas, star and snow flake due to their basis in relational models fail to adequately represent the semantics and operations of multi-dimensional data. There is always the problem of running complex (aggregate) queries on complex data. Also efficient execution of SQL queries is limited when drilling down in a data warehouse based on these models. The relatively new model/schema, star flake, which is the merger between the star and snowflake schema, manages to address some of these issues but fails to address all of them.

Later researchers, who adopted Object-Oriented techniques and Multidimensional data modelling for complex data, proposed many variations to the warehouse design. Many of the designs arise from the data mining On-Line Analytical Processing (OLAP) areas. Most of them concentrate on efficiency in query processing and data access rather than data semantics. Most of them were commercially unsuccessful as warehouse designs due to the "un-popularity" of Object-Oriented Database Management Systems (OODBMS) and limitations imposed by relational design constraints [1,2].

A data warehouse, primarily contains historical, consolidated data and should not lose its semantics at any point in time. But all methods suggested above are either non-semantically oriented or process oriented or a little bit of both. Almost all data warehouse models discussed above fail to capture the business side of the data warehouse. As a starting point, primary users of data warehouses are non-technical, middle and top end managers who have little or no knowledge of databases. No business rules can be captured inside the data warehouse. Most of the data warehouse designs are incapable of interpreting the business cost of data stored in them. As the business changes rapidly, the warehouses cannot or need complex query manipulation or re-design to accommodate the business changes. Though the data stored in them is historical, the information derived from them should accommodate the changes in the core business. At present the models above provide very little or no support for dynamic business information retrieval.

We are developing a methodology which utilizes current and new data warehouse design techniques to capture data semantics, business rules and business cost associated with each piece of information stored in or retrieved from the data warehouse. The new warehouse design will be based on the Object-Relational data model due to its ability to (1) capture both dynamic and static aspect of data ware houses, (2) utilize the growing O-R database market and (3) Semantic integration of data and systems.

4   Existing Data Warehouse Development Approaches

Several advanced approaches for dynamic data mart and virtualization for increased agility and reduced cost for Corporate Data Warehouse (CDW)/Business Intelligence (BI) applications include [6,7,16-18] and these are briefly discussed below:

1)   Federated, Multi-source Data Environment: A Data Virtualisation (DV) technology may access a data warehouse, in essence mirroring all of the existing consumable tables. DV can then extend this view to include other data to create a federated data capability. This can increase agility and reduce costs associated with physically moving data.

2)   Spatial Temporal Data Warehouse: it contains geographical data sets, moving objects, the notion of timespan/valid time, historical tracking etc. It is important to make sure that the DW supports spatial and temporal notions. Spatial data warehouses (SDW) rely on extended multidimensional (MD) models in order to provide decision makers with appropriate structures to explore spatial data by using different analysis techniques such as OLAP (On-Line Analytical Processing). Current development approaches are focused on defining a unique and static spatial multidimensional (SMD) schema at the conceptual level over which all decision makers fulfil their current spatial information needs [10].

A conceptual multidimensional model includes spatial dimensions, spatial fact relationships, spatial hierarchies, spatial measures, and topological relationships and operations. This extension provides a new conceptual model called the MultiDimER. The GeoDWFrame framework has been proposed in [12], which is built on the star schema and used as a guide to design spatial dimensional schemas. This framework has two types of dimensions. The first type is geographical, which is categorized into primitive and composed dimensions that have at all levels only spatial data such as customers addresses, geo-references. The second type is a hybrid that is grouped into micro, macro, and joint that deals with spatial and conventional data such as customer's addresses, geo-references, product valid time/time span etc.

3)   Virtual Data Marts: In this type data virtualization may augment CDW/BI by replacing some of the data marts with data virtualization objects (Views). A traditional DW might feed into virtual data marts, all within the DV platform. Again, such an approach can increase team agility and reduce costs associated with physically moving data. Such an architecture should be carefully vetted with a particular focus on performance.

4)   Real-Time Data Warehouse: The traditional data warehouse was designed to store and analyse historical information on the assumption that data would be captured now and analysed later. System architectures focused on scaling relational data up with larger hardware and processing to an operations schedule based on clean data. Yet the velocity of how data is captured, processed, and used is increasing. Companies are using real-time data to change, build, or optimize their businesses as well as to sell, transact, and engage in dynamic, event-driven processes like market trading [6].

To enable **real-time data acquisition**, Oracle GoldenGate [19] uses log-based, real-time CDC (Change Data Capture and Delivery) capabilities to provide continuous capture and delivery of the most recently changed data between OLTP systems and the data warehouse. CDC technologies identify and capture changes made to enterprise data sources, and then deliver those changes to target systems. The application offers transactional, real-time data capture, routing, transformations, and delivery, using the push approach. As soon as a new database transaction is committed at the source system, that data is immediately captured via the database transaction logs and moved to the data warehouse where it can drive enhanced, strategic, and operational BI capabilities.

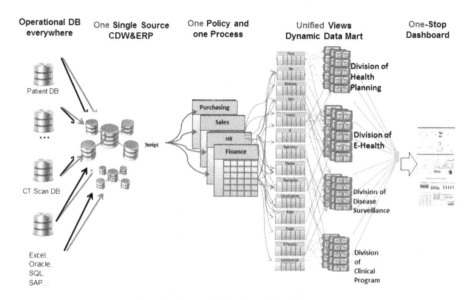

Fig. 2. Dynamic Data Mart Architecture

5   New Dynamic Data Mart Implementation Framework

5.1   The Dynamic Data Mart Implementation Architecture

The dynamic data mart as shown in Figure 2 and 3 has two layers, namely:

- The dimensional layer and sub-dimensional layer, in Green colour
- The dynamic fact tables, shown in blue colour that will be represented as a view. The view is realized through the user interface, such as a pop-up window, or a form, or a graph, etc.

As there is a close connection between Capability, Acquisition, Sustainment and Disposal, it is important to have integrated dimensions. This is to avoid each department or subsidiary having to create their own data mart and pull in only the data they need, resulting in having data centres and data marts everywhere.

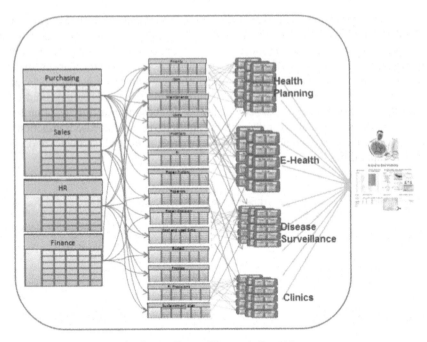

Fig. 3. The Heart of Dynamic Data Mart

5.2   The Underlining Principles of the Dynamism

The Dynamic Data Mart Engine is a forward and backward loop that carries out 3M and 3R functions, as shown in Figure 4.

3M, Namely:
Data Mining: mining the application log that mines the user's behaviours/user's decision making and usage rates of each view and window widgets clicks, providing usage rates.
Data Marshalling: for low usage rate views, we collect the data set, put them on a probation period, to see whether we can reuse.
Data Meshing: based on the data mining and data marshalling report, we create new views that potentially will attract the usage.

3R, Namely:
Recommendation: Following up 3M, we provide recommendations to the user, in an analogous manner to how Amazon.com gives recommendations to people who have purchased a book by recommending them other similar books that other people have bought, that are likely to use the similar data set and make similar decisions, but this decision making is now recorded and reused.
Reconciliation: If the data is likely useful with high hit rate, but the view is not useful to finish a task, we reconcile all the window widgets and data sets to provide new window workflows or widgets workflows.
Representation: We then represent a new view to replace the old view to the user.

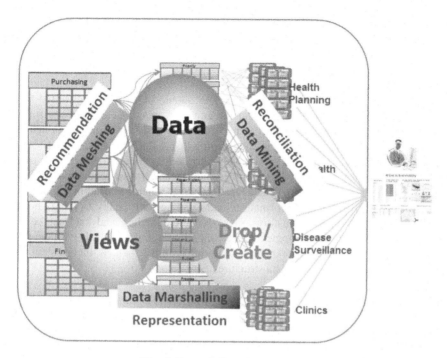

Fig. 4. Dynamic Data Mart Engine

5.3   User Behaviour Mining, Log Mining and Usage Mining

We track the logs from a configured user's windows. The dashboard shows a number of areas, for each area we track the number sessions, the number of distinct users, peak concurrent sessions, cumulative duration of sessions and a user ratio.

Our 3M3R engine analyses peak concurrency events, solution adoption, decision making process, most active users (and candidates for Named Cals), and it drills down to individual session details (sessions tab) at each Window Area. It uses the trend chart on the concurrency tab to drill down to a minute level of detail.

The framework allows us to track how many times users open the model through the server log files and which user accessed the dashboard. By using Audit Logging we can track which objects and tabs are accessed by users and to perform this on the server the option Enable audit log has to be selected.

6   Dynamic Data Mart Implementation

6.1   Staging

STAGE 1 : CDW Data Dumps / Data Replication

A Corporate Data warehouse system contains various information system's database dumps. Currently, these database dumps are not consumed by any software application but for the dynamic DM technology we are going to use them to build a data warehouse. It is important to note that these database dumps are developed using various technologies such as Microsoft SQL Server 2008, IBM DB2, Excel Files Text files etc.

STAGE 2 : Data Progression
The data stored in the database dumps in CDW should be extracted, cleansed to remove inconsistencies and fill gaps, and integrated to merge heterogeneous sources into one common schema. In order to achieve this, the first step is different databases integration by defining global schema and storing this in the Meta-Data Repository. In a multiple database system, a global schema created by integrating schemas of the individual databases that provides a uniform interface and high level location transparency for the users to retrieve data. Once the global schema is established, the next step is to use Extraction, Transformation, and Loading tools (ETL) to merge heterogeneous schemata, extract, transform, cleanse, validate, filter, and load source data into a data warehouse. Technologically speaking, the staging area deals with the problems that are typical for different databases integration, such as inconsistent data management and incompatible data structures.

STAGE 3: From Corporate Data Warehouse to Dynamic Data Marts (Dynamic DM)
As a result of ETL processes, the Information extracted and transformed will be located to one logically centralized single repository: a corporate data warehouse (CDW). During analysis and design of the data warehouse, various dimensions and facts tables will be identified according to faceplate requirements. These dimensions and facts tables will be loaded with the cleansed, transformed data created as a result of ETL process. The CDW will be used as a source for creating data marts such as Subsidiary 1...n, which partially replicate data warehouse contents and are designed for specific subsidiaries. Meta-data repositories store information on sources, access procedures, data staging, users, data mart schemata, and so on.

STAGE 4: User's Dashboard
Once the integrated data is efficiently and flexibly accessed to the user friendly Dynamic Data Mart and GUIs (Graphical User Interfaces), managers will be able to analyse items listed according to priorities, they will be able to dynamically analyse individual item/platform details, and will be able to simulate business scenarios. The Dynamic DM will be equipped with descriptive, predictive and prescriptive analytics models that will help managers to better visualize the pool size, history, forecast lead times and asset life etc.

6.2   ELT: Extract, Load, and Transform for Dynamic DM

In order to create the Dynamic Data Mart, we start with ELT:

1. Extract the data from the operational databases and load them into a corporate database (dump database).
2. Transform the data from the dump database into data marts (SQL scripts or other type of scripting)

3. Define the fact measure and connection to dimensions in order to create the fact tables and views.
4. Apply BI service on the Views.

6.3   The Dimension Tables and Fact Tables

In Data warehousing, the dimension table contains the textual or descriptive attributes of the data. For example, Customer dimension will contain details about customer's name, address, phone number etc.

Dimensions are used to slice and dice the data i.e. filter and group the data. Dimensional table which also help you by looking at data with "By" attribute i.e. say if the Total sales of the company is $1 Million then using Customer dimension you can look at the Total sales "By" Customer or "By" Time. A dimension table has a primary key column also called Dimension ID/Dim Id that uniquely identifies each dimension row. The dimension table is associated with a fact table using this key.

Fact Table contains the measurable attributes of the data. It contains measurable data that can be analysed by Dimension tables. Fact tables contain the foreign keys of the associated Dimension tables (figure 5).

6.4   The Data Model to Represent Fact and Dimension

The data model is used to develop dynamic association between fact tables and dimensions and its sub-dimensions. This allows self-organized Business Intelligence by providing automated easy drill-down operation for the end-user with automated data association.

Data Association is a technology that is widely used in modern BI tools, that builds the relationship between the concepts, and between the entities or tables, or between data-sets.

We create the Dynamic Data Mart with Dynamic Dimensions, Dynamic Tables and Dynamic Views.

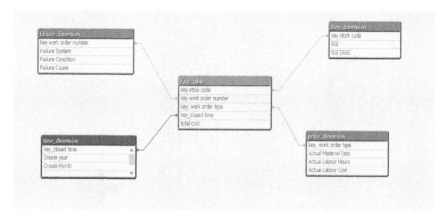

Fig. 5. The Dynamic Data Model Sample

6.5   Dynamic Create and Drop Views and Data

Once we have the data on which dimensions are not used, we link this data to a new fact table named unused views and/or directly load the data to a dashboard in order to rank and visualize the views the least used.

Therefore we can choose to drop the views automatically if they are not used for more than 2 months (for example) or we let an IT manager decide if the views should be dropped. In the same way we can automatically create views knowing which data users accessed the most.

The automatic part would be created using an external application linked to our BI software or using a script inside our BI software if it is powerful enough. Using the data about usage ("name"; "number of times used"), a simple formula targeting views can be used such as: with usage less than A=? and more than B=?. Then, we can create or delete views by linking the targeted views to the BI software (Figure 6).

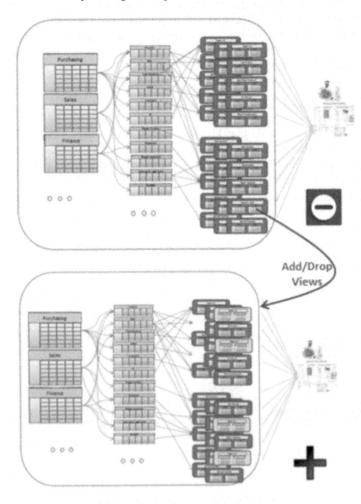

Fig. 6. User Behaviour and usage mining, create/drop views

7   Application of Dynamic Data Mart

7.1   View Design and User Operation

We design the screens with partitions. All areas are linked together: we can know which area is the most used for changing all the dashboard (selection bookmark) but not which area is useful or useless. Indeed, an area could be good for visualizing information but not for selecting information and thus would appear as if it was never used. A solution could be to create a usage table where every time a data is changed on an area it adds one on "number of time used" (low number would mean it is not an important area). However, it would not be accurate since we do not know whether the user is using all the areas modified because most of them are linked together.

In addition, we will track down all the pop-ups, all the mouse clicks, and all the window widget. The steps involved include:

- Screen Design and partition for automated usability tracking
- USE OF SCRIPTS TO CREATE DIMENSIONS AND SUB-DIMENSIONS
- USE OF SCRIPTS TO CREATE FACTS TABLES
- USE OF SCRIPTS TO CREATE DATA MART
- MAP DYNAMIC DM TO USER'S DASHBOARD

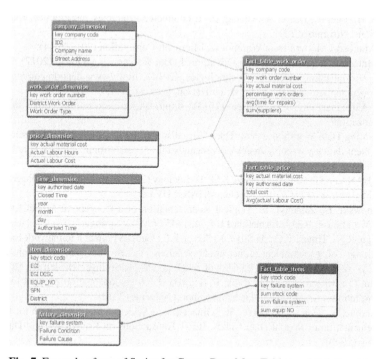

Fig. 7. Example of use of Script for Create Data Mart Tables and Relationship

8   Conclusion

The paper examines the state of the art of Data Warehouses and how they are aligned with the company's processes. There is a strong need for Data Integration from multiple Data Sources and its effective use to answer questions posed by people in the business at different levels plus effective presentation in a form to which these business users can relate. A major weakness of current Data Warehouse and Data Mart approaches is the lack of adaptability so that evolution of the company's processes and Data requirements as well as new Business Questions can be addressed. This paper present an approach based on Dynamic Data Mart to overcome these weaknesses.

References

1. Rahayu, J.W., Chang, E., Dillon, T.S., Taniar, D.: Performance Evaluation of The Object-Relational transformation methodology. Data Knowledge Engineering **38**(3), 265–300 (2001)
2. Rahayu, J.W., Chang, E., Dillon, T.S., Taniar, D.: A methodology for transforming inheritance relationships in an object-oriented conceptual model to relational tables. Information & Software Technology **42**(8), 571–592 (2000)
3. Chan, H., Lee, R., Dillon, T., Chang, E.: E-commerce Principles and Practice. John Wiley and Sons, November 2001
4. The Microsoft Modern Data Warehouse, Microsoft Corporation (2013/2014)
5. Data Integration Architectures for Operational Data Warehousing. Oracle (2012)
6. Data Virtualisation, Denodo Technologies (2014). http://www.denodo.com/en/system/files/document-attachments/data_virtualization_goes_mainstream.pdf
7. Data Virtualisation, Data Source (2013). http://datasourceconsulting.com/8-steps-data-virtualization/
8. Integrating Data Warehouse with Data Virtualisation. Intel (2013). http://www.intel.com.au/content/dam/www/public/us/en/documents/white-papers/virtualization-integrating-data-warehouses-for-bi-agility-paper.pdf
9. SAP HANA and Data Virtualisation. SAP Technology (2012). http://stats.manticoretechnology.com/ImgHost/582/12917/2012/Resources/HANA-DV.pdf
10. Malinowski, E., Zimányi, E.: Logical Representation of a Conceptual Model for Spatial Data Warehouses. GeoInformatica **11**(4), 431–457 (2007). Springer
11. Fidalgo, R.N., Times, V.C., da Silva, J., Souza, F.F.: GeoDWFrame: a framework for guiding the design of geographical dimensional schemas. In: Kambayashi, Y., Mohania, M., Wöß, W. (eds.) DaWaK 2004. LNCS, vol. 3181, pp. 26–37. Springer, Heidelberg (2004)
12. Glorio, O., Mazón, J.-N., Garrigós, I., Trujillo, J.: A personalization process for spatial data warehouse development. Decision Support Systems (2012)
13. Stefanovic, N., Han, J., Koperski, K.: Object-Based Selective Materialization for Efficient Implementation of Spatial Data Cubes. IEEE Transactions on Knowledge and Data Engineering (2000)
14. Kern, R., Stolarczyk, T., Nguyen, N.T.: A formal framework for query decomposition and knowledge integration in data warehouse federations. Expert Systems Applications **40** (2013)

15. Jarke, M., List, T., Koller, J.: The Challenge of Process Data Warehousing. VLDB conference (2000)
16. Gartner, Magic Quadrant Data Warehouse Data Management Solutions for Analytics (2015)
17. Gartner, Magic Quadrant for Data Quality Tools (2014)
18. ThoughtWeb, Logical Data Warehousing for Big Data (2013)
19. Data Integration Architectures for Operational Data Warehousing. Oracle (2012)

ANOVA Based Approch for Efficient Customer Recognition: Dealing with Common Names

Morteza Saberi[1(✉)] and Zahra Saberi[2]

[1] School of Business, UNSW Canberra, Canberra BC 2610, Australia
m.saberi.ie@gmail.com
[2] School of Industrial Engineering, University of Tehran, Tehran, Iran

Abstract. This study proposes an Analysis of Variance (ANOVA) technique that focuses on the efficient recognition of customers with common names. The continuous improvement of Information and communications technologies (*ICT*) has led customers to have new expectations and concerns from their related organization. These new expectations bring various difficulties for organizations' help desk to meet their customers' needs. In this paper, we propose a technique that provides the most beneficial information to the Customer service representative that will assist in the efficient recognition of the customer. The proposed algorithm determines which features of a customer should be asked that would result in his/her prompt recognition. Moreover, to have a clean database, the framework uses the features of customers for which a standard format is available such as street address, month of birth etc. We evaluate our algorithm on synthetic dataset and demonstrate how we can recognize the right customer in the optimum manner.

Keywords: Contact centres · Customer recognition · Customer common name

1 Introduction

Customer relationship management (CRM) is a framework for managing a company's interactions with current and future customers [1, 2]. In this highly competitive world, it is essential for every organization to have an efficient and smart CRM system. One important part of CRM system is contact center which is in direct contact with the customers. Contact center has been termed as the new version of call centers which allow customers to express their queries via different communication channels: telephone, touch-point telephone, fax, letter, email and online live chat [3]. However, for the contact centers to be effective, they need to be able to identify the customers in question from their database efficiently and effectively. To achieve that, in this study a framework is proposed that utilizes the ANOVA technique to assist contact centers with efficient customer recognition which using telephone and online live chat as the main communication channels.

Currently, individuals are in contact with organization via diverse communication channels [4]. This diversity has two impacts: increasing easiness and flexibility of communication and producing dirty data [5]. The first one is beneficial for the

© IFIP International Federation for Information Processing 2015
T. Dillon (Ed.): IFIP AI 2015, IFIP AICT 465, pp. 64–74, 2015.
DOI: 10.1007/978-3-319-25261-2_6

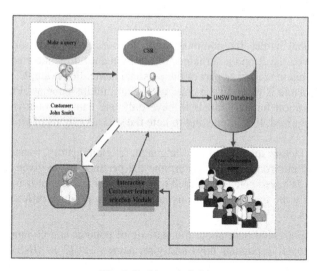

Fig. 1. Problem definition

customers while the second one can be a risk for the efficient working of a CRM system. Performance of CRM systems is decreased by existence of dirty data in them. Another issue with CRM system is that customers have different IDs from different organizations. It should be noted that they do not normally memorize all of their IDs. From a psychological perspective, customers prefer to be recognized by their name as their identity, not by a customer number or ID number. The feeling of ownership achieved from a name is much greater than that achieved from address, phone number etc. In some cultures, people who have nicknames prefer to use them as their official given names. Recognizing customers using their name is not a difficult task if the same or similar names are not available in the organization database. However, the recognition is difficult when there are common names in the CRM database. As an example, 7.4% of family name in china is 'Li' and by considering 1 milliard as the china population it is 74 million individuals with "Li" as the family name [6]

In the current study, we have focused on customer recognition in the case of existence of the common name in CRM database by making use of ANOVA Based Approach. The main aim of the proposed algorithm is to recognize the customer by asking the minimum number of questions with them. The output of the algorithm is a sequence of most informative questions (customer features) that needs to be asked from the customer. It achieves this by using two sources of information: customer record(s) in organization database and customer interactions (answer) with the CSR (or: information provided by customers in their interaction) The proposed framework links the customer interactions (responses) with the organization database in order to fulfill customer recognition task. The first data source of information (CRM database) can contain noisy and dirty data.

The paper is organized as follows: Section 2 defines the problem along with a discussion on common name issue for contact centers. The framework of ANOVA based approach for efficient customer recognition is explained in Section 3.

2   Common Names

Individuals use their personal names for communication purposes [6]. A personal name usually includes a given name and a surname (or family name). In some countries and cultures, a middle name is used as part of the personal name. For example, in Brazil the mother's family name is given to the child as his/her middle name at birth. In some countries, it is common for individuals to have only one name (mononymous) by which they are recognized. It is interesting to note the various origins of given names:

It is evident that various factors such as culture, language, religion, history, translation to a new language, and environment may determine the personal name given to an individual [7]. These fields have been also studied by researchers and are known as Anthroponymy study. Briefly the mentioned various factors lead to produce different variations of personal names.

Figures. Some figures are presented here about the statistic of popular and common name. Table 1 shows the top five popular boys and girls name in 2013 in UNSW, Australia. It is clear even within a given state the number of common name is high. This issue is more severe in countries such china. As an example, 7.4% of family name in china is 'Li' and by considering 1 milliard as the china population it is 74 million individuals with "Li" as the family name.   Some organization such as health care, insurance, telecommunications company that have high number of customer are more faced with the issue of common name.

Table 1. Popular Baby Names in UNSW 2013

Boys	Number	Girls	Number
William	696	Charlotte	613
Oliver	630	Olivia	551
Jack	574	Amelia	540
Noah	555	Chloe	517
James	510	Mia	517

3   ANOVA Based Approch for Efficient Customer Recognition

This section presents the general framework of interactive customer feature selection. This framework assists CRM systems with customer recognition when the system faces the common name issue. The proposed framework relies on two integrated modules as shown in Figure 1.

Analysis of Variance(ANOVA) is developed by Fisher to find out whether is it any difference among groups average [7]. We performed ANOVA on customer standard features to find if means of these features are statistically different or not. Null hypothesis can be accepted or rejected by performing ANOVA F-test in a consequence. We use average of feature values as the index for selecting the first question if ANOVA shows no difference among standard features (Null Hypothesis acceptance). Also if the null hypothesis in ANOVA F-test is rejected, multiple pair comparison is performed to find the *most informative question*. Before presenting the proposed *Duncan's multiple range test (*DMRT) based algorithm in a formal way it has been explained with the following three examples.

Example 1. This example shows how we select the first question when the null hypothesis is rejected. A multiple pair comparison is performed in this case, as shown in Table 2. The number of rejections associated with each feature is highlighted in Table 3. As the maximum number belongs to Street, it has been selected in this example. This maximum number is the reason that Street is the source of rejection in the null hypothesis.

Table 2. Multiple pair comparison example with 1 hypothesis acceptance

Null Hypothesis & Pairwise Comparisons	Decision	Selected Question
$\mu_{street} = \mu_{suburb} = \mu_{Month}$	reject	
$\mu_{street} = \mu_{suburb}$	reject	
$\mu_{street} = \mu_{Month}$	reject	
$\mu_{suburb} = \mu_{Month}$	accept	**Street**

Table 3. Associated Number of rejection for customer features in Multiple pair comparison test (Example)

Feature	Number of rejection
Street	2
Suburb	1
Month of Birth	1

Example 2. Examination of Table 4, *as the second example*, shows the first question could be determined between **Street & Suburb** in this case. From statistical viewpoint customers month values are not different (statistically) with Street and suburb and the *most informative question* should be determined from **Street & Suburb**. Also number of rejections for these two features is equal as mentioned in Table 5.

Table 4. Multiple pair comparison example with 2 hypothesis acceptances

Null Hypothesis & Pairwise Comparisons	Decision	Selected Question
$\mu_{street} = \mu_{suburb} = \mu_{Month}$	reject	
$\mu_{street} = \mu_{suburb}$	reject	
$\mu_{street} = \mu_{Month}$	accept	
$\mu_{suburb} = \mu_{Month}$	accept	**Street, Suburb**

Table 5. Associated Number of rejection for customer features in Multiple pair comparison test

Feature	Number of rejection
Street	1
Suburb	1
Month of Birth	0

Example 3. In Table 6, we have the case in which three attribute are nominated after performing multiple pair comparison. As in Table 7 stated the number of rejection for all customer features is equal

Table 6. Multiple pair comparison example with 3 hypothesis rejections

Null Hypothesis & Pairwise Comparisons	Decision	Selected Question(s)
$\mu_{street} = \mu_{suburb}$ $= \mu_{Month}$	reject	
$\mu_{street} = \mu_{suburb}$	reject	**Street,**
$\mu_{street} = \mu_{Month}$	reject	**Suburb,** **Month**
$\mu_{suburb} = \mu_{Month}$	reject	

Table 7. Associated Number of rejection for customer features in Multiple pair comparison test

Feature	Number of rejection
Street	2
Suburb	2
Month of Birth	2

Now we should answer this question:

How we should determine the optimum attribute in case of two or three nominated attributes?

As formally P-value shows how rejection or acceptance is strong, we use this value to come up to the best question (attribute). We utilize this nature of P-value that *the more P-value distance with confidence levels the more robust statistical rejection.* The detailed mathematical presentation of this approach has been explained later.

A.   Analysis of Variance Based Algorithm Formal Definition

In the previous section we have provided intuitive example that shows how ANOVA approach help us to find the *most informative question.* We have two main hypothesis regarding ANOVA usage in customer recognition. The null hypothesis assume the statistically equality of all customer profile features average and on the other hand alternative hypothesis assume average of customer profile features are different. If null hypothesis is rejected then we are in need of finding the cause of this rejection. The feature that leads to this rejection (inequality of features average) is the *most informative question* and should be asked from the customer. Lines 3 to 18 in Figure 1 shows how find the cause of this rejection. When we get rejection the multiple pair comparison test is then performed and based on number of rejection that is associated with each feature the first feature is selected. The detail of selection is highlighted in the algorithm. Also the process of finding sequence of questions has been depicted in next section. In ANOVA based algorithm some functions have been used as their task are listed in Table 8.

	ANOVA based algorithm (A)
	Input: A set of records with standard features A,
	Number of rows (A) m, ANOVA F-test **ANOVA**;
	Output: preferable feature
	$T \leftarrow$ **Distance**(A);
1	$H \leftarrow$ **ANOVA**(T);
2	**If (H=1)**
3	$M \leftarrow Mul\_Comp(T, \alpha)$ $L \leftarrow N\_Rejection(M)$
5	$z \leftarrow Maximal\_Index(L)$
6	**If (size(z)<2)**
7	**Return** $Feature_z$; **Else if (size(z)==2)**
8	$x \leftarrow$ **Max_Distance**$(T|z)$
9	**Return** $Feature_x$
10	**Else**
12	$x \leftarrow max\_dif\_Pvalue(M|z)$, $k \leftarrow size(x)$
14	**If k=1**
15	**Return** $Feature_x$
16	**Else** $y \leftarrow$ **max_distance**$(T|x)$, **Return** $Feature_y$
17	End
18	End
19	**Else**
20	$y \leftarrow$ **max_distance**$(T|x)$, **Return** $Feature_y$
21	End

Fig. 2. ANOVA algorithm

Table 8. ANOVA Algorithm functions definition

function	description
$T \leftarrow$ Distance(A)	Return the matrix T that is average distance of correspondent member of A from other members in its column
ANOVA (T)	Perform ANOVA F-test and determine the acceptance or rejection status of Null Hypothesis. If test reject the null hypothesis then the H is equal to 1.
$M \leftarrow$ Mul_Comp (T, α)	Perform multiple pair comparison on T and returns a matrix M of pairwise comparison results with α confidence level.
$L \leftarrow N\_Rejection(M)$	Return dataset array L that shows the number of rejection which each feature got in total pairs.
$z \leftarrow Maximal\_Index(L)$	Returns indices of the maximum values of L in output vector z.
Max_Distance (T/z):	Returns indices of features which the distance between its string values is the maximum (maximal) in comparison with other features.
Max_dif_Pvalue(M/z):	first calculate the difference between p-value and critical value and find index(es) with the maximum(maximal) value(s). The detail about this function has been highlighted in Figure.

In the following figures (2-4), procedures of finding out the three functions are explained: *Distance, Max_Distance* and *Max_dif_Pvalue.*

---

distance(A)

> **Input:** A set of records with standard features *A*,
>
> Number of rows (A) *m*, Normalized levenshtein distance ***Leven***;
>
> **Output:** Distance of matrix A member from others
>
> $$distance_j = Average_{i \neq h}(Normalized\_Leven(A(i,j), A(h,j)))$$
>
> **Return** *distance*;

Fig. 3. Distance function

Max_distance(A|z)

> **Input:** A set of records with standard features *A*,
>
> Number of rows (A) *m*, ;
>
> **Output:** indices of the maximum distances among each feature
>
> **For** $j \in z$: $(A|z) \leftarrow A - A(:,j)$ **End**
>
> $dist_j = distance(A|z)$
>
> $j^* \leftarrow arg\_max_j(dist_j)$
>
> **Return** j^*;

Fig. 4. Max_Distance function

Max_dif_Pvalue(M|z)

> **Input:** A set of records with standard features *A*,
>
> Number of rows (A) *m*, Normalized levenshtein distance ***Leven***;
>
> **Output:** indices of the maximum difference of P-value and confidence level
>
> $$dif\_pvalue_j = \sum_{i \neq j} |p_{value}(i,j) - 0.05| \quad ; i \in z \, \& \, M(i,j)=0$$
>
> $i^* \leftarrow arg\_max_j(dif\_pvalue_j)$
>
> **Return** j^*;

Fig. 5. Max_dif_Pvalue function

B.   Generating Sequence of Questions by Using ANOVA Algorithm: Formal Definition

The way of generating sequence of questions by using ANOVA is explained here. As it is stated in line 14 (Figure 5), when we have two remained feature then we select the question by using ***Max_distance*** function. Actually when we have two features using ANOVA test is meaningless and we just used simply edit distance metric. The feature with highest distance among its values is selected with this function. To have a better follow up the example has been given here as well that shows how the sequence of questions is generated in ANOVA approach.

	Algorithm_ANOVA(Customer Name)
	Input: X as common name, a set of records with Name (X) A, List of Common names C, number of customer standard features n, a set of standard features Z, Successful customer recognition **flag**;
	Output: Sequence of questions (features) SQ
1	$IF\ Y \in C\ THEN$
2	Break
3	Else $X \leftarrow Y$ End
4	$A \leftarrow Records\ with\ name\ X$
5	$flag, i \leftarrow 0$
7	**While** flag $==0$
8	$k \leftarrow n - i$
9	If (k>2)
10	$Q^* \leftarrow ANOVA(A)$
11	$SQ(i) \leftarrow Q^*;\ Z \leftarrow Z - \{Q^*\}$
13	Else
14	$Q^* \leftarrow$ **Max_distance**$(A|z)$
15	$SQ(i) \leftarrow Q^*$
16	End
17	$flag \leftarrow$ **Recognition**(A, k^*, p)
18	$i \leftarrow i + 1$
19	End
20	$A \leftarrow$ Records with $SQ(i)$ customer answer
21	**If** i==n
22	Go to **20**
23	**End**
24	Go to **9**
25	Ask sequence of other features
26	**END**
27	**Return SQ;**

Fig. 6. ANOVA Based Approach pseudo-code

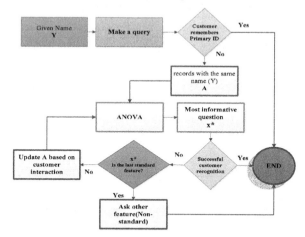

Fig. 7. Generating sequence of questions by using ANOVA algorithm

Figure 6 also depicts flowchart of generating sequence of questions by using ANOVA algorithm.

C.   Example

We show how ANOVA based algorithm finds Mary Miller profile which is mentioned in Table 9. As stated in Table 10 by performing ANOVA F-test, Null Hypothesis is rejected and we should do the multiple comparisons test to find the sequence of questions.

Table 9. Generating sequence of questions' dataset example

	Customer Name	Street	Suburb	Month of Birth
1	Mary Miller	South Guildford	Donnelly River	June
2	Mary Miller	Hart close	Dural	July
3	Mary Miller	Neerabup	Doodenanning	July
4	Mary Miller	Nollamara	Doongin	April
5	Mary Miller	Noranda	Daadenning Creek	January
6	Mary Miller	North Beach	Dagger Hills	May
7	Mary Miller	Stuart	Palmerston	September
8	Mary Miller	Stuart	Palmerston	October
9	Mary Miller	Stuart	Palmerston	September
10	Mary Miller	South Guildford	Donnelly River	November
11	Mary Miller	Preston	Emu phlains	December
12	Mary Miller	Preston	Emu phlains	April
13	Mary Miller	South Guildford	West Ballidu	January

Table 10. Null Hypothesis ANOVA F-test performing multiple comparisons

Null Hypothesis	Decision	P-value
$\mu_{street} = \mu_{suburb} = \mu_{Month}$	reject	2.20E-08

Result of Multiple comparisons test can be obtained from Table 11. Rejection (**1**) or acceptance (**0**) and associated p-values are reported in this table. As number of rejections is equal for all three features (Table 12) the P-value is employed to determine the first question. According to the reported values in Table 13, **Month** is the first question that should asked from **John**.

Table 11. Multiple comparisons result with correspondent P-Values

	Street	Suburb	Month
Street	0	**1,** 0.0049	**1,** 2.1404e-006
Suburb	**1,** 0.0049	0	**1,** 8.2137e-007
Month of Birth	**1,** 2.1404e-006	**1,** 8.2137e-007	0

Table 12. Associated Number of rejection for customer features in Multiple pair comparison test

Feature	Number of rejection
Street	2
Suburb	2
Month of Birth	2

Table 13. Max_dif_Pvalue results

Feature	Value
Street	0.9951
Suburb	0.9951
Month of Birth	1.0000

As *John's* month of birth is *July*, we come up with the following updated records (Table 14). As we have just two remaining features the next question is selected by using *Max_distance* function. Examination of Table 15 shows the next question is *John's* Street address.

As *John's* month of birth is *July*, we come up with the following updated records (Table 14). As we have just two remained feature the next question is selected by using *Max_distance* function. Examination of Table 15 shows the next question is *John's* Street address.

Table 14. Updated dataset based on customer answer

	Street	Suburb	Month of Birth
2	Hart close	Dural	July
3	Neerabup	Doodenanning	July

Table 15. Max_distance function Result

Feature	Value
Street	0.9
Suburb	0.83

SQ=(Month, Street)

4   Conclusion

This study present an interactive customer feature selection to deal with common variations in personal names. Three algorithms from different schools of thoughts, information retrieval, machine learning, and statistical analysis, to find the optimum sequence of questions. These algorithms are IDF and Levenshtein based , C4.5 based and ANOVA based. The preferred approach is the one which require the minimum number of customer interactions. About 60000 records as the synthetic data are used to show the applicability of the proposed framework. Febrl software as the data generator used various parameters that these let get more insights from the framework's operation. The unique features of the proposed framework enable it to: have online responses, deal with common names, improve the cleansing of the database, have faster performance. The preferred algorithm is selected fast and smooth recognition. The framework has been designed so that it improves the cleansing quality of the CRM system database (customer"s data); a clean database improves performance and subsequently leads to better customer satisfaction.

References

1. Faed, A.: An Intelligent Customer Complaint Management System with Application to the Transport and Logistics Industry. Springer Science & Business (2013)
2. http://www.coveo.com/en/news-releases/Coveo-survey-shows-organizations-falling-short-in-generating-insight-from-unstructured-content
3. Saberi, O.K.H.M.: Intelligent online customer recognition framework: dealing with common personal names. In: ICIEA 2014, China (2014)
4. Pan, S.L., Lee, J.-N.: Using e-CRM for a unified view of the customer. Communications of the ACM **46**(4), 95–99 (2003)
5. Hussain, O.K., Chang, E., Ramakonar, V., Dillon, T.S.: A Customer Relationship Management ecosystem that utilizes multiple sources and types of information conjointly, pp. 1–6
6. Saberi, M., Hussain, O.K., Janjua, N.K., Chang, E.-J.: In-house crowdsourcing-based entity resolution: dealing with common names, pp. 83–88
7. Fisher, R.A.: Studies in Crop Variation. I. An examination of the yield of dressed grain from Broadbalk. The Journal of Agricultural Science **11**(02), 107–135 (1921)

Wholesale Power to Hydrogen: Adaptive Trading Approaches in a Smart Grid Ecosystem

Serkan Özdemir$^{(\boxtimes)}$ and Rainer Unland

DAWIS, University of Duisburg-Essen, Schützenbahn 70, 45127 Essen, Germany
{serkan.oezdemir,rainer.unland}@icb.uni-due.de

Abstract. Fossil based liquid fuels, primarily used in transportation systems, are likely to be replaced with renewable resources thanks to energy transition policies. However, shifting from stable energy production (using coal, natural gas) to highly volatile renewable production will bring a number of problems as well. On the other side, tremendous developments in solar and wind power technologies encourage energy investors to maximize their contributions over the electricity grid. This highly volatile energy resources bring a strong research question to the attention: How to benefit from excess energy? Power-to-gas seems to be a strong candidate to store excess energy. Besides, power-to-hydrogen is seen as a liquid fuel for fuel cell vehicles. This paper aims to analyze trading approaches of a power-to-hydrogen system to minimize the energy costs. To achieve that, Markov Decision Process (MDP) along with Q-learning is modelled as well as a number of trading approaches. This research aims to reveal the feasibility of hydrogen as a fuel option in future smart grid.

Keywords: Trading · Hydrogen · Transportation · Simulation · Power to gas

1 Introduction

Due to energy transition policies of governments and recent developments in renewable energy technologies, fossil and nuclear based power plants tend to be replaced with renewable resources. Recent developments show that the number of installed capacity will dramatically increase in the near future. Solar siding and roof-top panel technologies are rapidly growing since they have a large footprint compared to other renewable resources. This work assumes that energy transition will shift towards renewables as already planned by many countries.

In case of high renewable penetration, future smart grid will face with a number of challenges, such as meeting the supply and demand in balance. Since the renewable energy production is highly weather-depended, a distributed energy storage is needed at off-peak hours or days to benefit from excess energy. Among other storage options, power-to-gas has the most storage capacity over other technologies [1][9][15]. The first step product of power-to-gas, obtained through electrolysis process, can be used as fuel in fuel cell vehicles. This way is more efficient than methane in terms of energy loss. Hydrogen is also nature friendly fuel and the output of fuel cell vehicles is only water. However hydrogen cannot be delivered to far away due to high pressure problems. For

© IFIP International Federation for Information Processing 2015
T. Dillon (Ed.): IFIP AI 2015, IFIP AICT 465, pp. 75–82, 2015.
DOI: 10.1007/978-3-319-25261-2_7

this reason, on-site production is one of the proposed methods for hydrogen production [8][9][11].

Fuel cells are usually considered as a competitor of battery electric vehicles. However, fuel cell vehicles are replacement of traditional combustion engine vehicles. Moreover, fuel cells are also battery electric vehicles. In addition to all functionalities of battery electric vehicles, fuel cells have high pressure hydrogen tank and fuel cell stack which converts hydrogen into electricity. For this reason, fuel cells can be solution to charging, efficiency and driving-range problems of battery electric vehicles.

This works aims to analyze hydrogen production through electrolysis process on the city level. Power Trading Agent Competition (Power TAC) is selected to simulate future smart grid conditions [16]. A hydrogen station is designed as a server module in which a number of fuel cell and conventional vehicles are simulated. Refilling station consists of an electrolysis unit, high pressure storage unit, dispensers and on-site renewable resources. The station is an active participant of a local wholesale market. The wholesale market is a typical hour-ahead market which allows participants to submit orders 24 hours prior to delivery. Proposed Markov Decision model and trading approaches are explained in Section 3.

2   State of the Art

Both power-to-hydrogen (PtH$_2$) and fuel cells are quite old concepts. Basically, the electrolysis extracts water into oxygen and hydrogen (H$_2$O $\rightarrow$ H$_2$ + O). Among different electrolysis approaches, alkaline electrolysis is the most common one in use. Conversion efficiency rate depends on the load, but the typical rate is 60-70% at full load. Hydrogen can be also injected into natural gas grid [14]. In a typical PtH$_2$ power plant, investment and operation-management costs have severe roles on the profitability of the plant. Following table shows the basic inputs and outputs of a PtH$_2$ power plant.

Table 1. Inputs and Outputs of a PtH$_2$ power plant and fuel station.

	Today	2030
Investment (electrolysis) (IC$_e$) [8]	1750 EUR / kW$_{input}$	700 EUR / kW$_{input}$
Investment (refueling st. + storage) (IC$_{rs}$) [3]	16 % of IC$_e$	8 % of IC$_e$
Operational costs [10]	3% of IC$_e$ + IC$_{rs}$	
Water consumption	0.2 l/kW$_{input}$	
Hydrogen production	1 kg / 48 kW	-0.492
Oxygen output	6 kg / 48 kW	-1.281
Useful heat	11 % of input.	
Wholesale market fees	15000-25000 EUR/year [7,8]	
Recurring market and grid fees, taxes	0.1-0.2 EUR/MWh	Possible incentives.

Besides the advantages of CO$_2$ emission level and driving range, fuel cells also performs a promising well-to-wheel performance for the future transportation. Following table compares roughly the well-to-wheel performances of fuel cell vehicles, battery electric vehicles and diesel vehicles.

Table 2. Comparison of different fuel types. Reference vehicles are B segment economy cars of Mercedes, Toyota and Hyundai.

	Fuel Cell Vehicle	Battery Electric vehicle	Diesel Vehicle
Range (100 km)	1 kg H$_2$ (48 kWh el. input)	18 kWh	5 liter
Well-to-wheel wholesale[1]	1.2 EUR	0.62 EUR	2.9 EUR [2]
Well-to-wheel retail	9 EUR [4]	4.68 EUR [5]	5.75 EUR [6]

There are a number of possible incentives that are subject to PtH$_2$ plants. However, on the legal side, some are not matured due to uncertainties on the future fuel options. But the good news is, there are many ongoing acts regarding to hydrogen fuel utilizing renewable electricity. Currently, many companies, such as OMV, Hydrogenics, Toyota and e-on are active in the hydrogen business by producing fuel cell cars, power plants and refilling stations.

On the other side, energy markets have the vital role on power-to-gas power plants and will be more important in the future due to high fluctuations. In the current situation, electric vehicles are exposed to retailer prices since it is not possible for each electric vehicle to trade in wholesale markets. Unlike electric vehicles, power-to-gas power plants and their refilling stations are able to trade in energy markets. For this reason, fuel cell transportation is seen as one of the strongest candidates for the future transportation system.

3   Methodology

In order to analyze hydrogen as a fuel option, a Power TAC server module is created. This module simulates a hydrogen refilling station and on-site hydrogen production. Local wholesale market and on-site renewables are electricity resources of hydrogen production. Note that Power TAC is simulated on the city level with a population of about 50 thousand residents, which fits to on-site PtH$_2$ power plant scenario since the long-haul distribution of hydrogen is not possible [14]. Figure 1 illustrates the schematic landscape of proposed environment.

The Power Trading Agent Competition (Power TAC) is an open source smart grid simulation platform which consists of wholesale market, tariff market, distribution utility and a number of costumer and producer models. Besides, autonomous brokers are allowed to trade remotely in these markets. The wholesale market is a typical hour-ahead market where the large generator companies, renewable production farms and brokers place their bids and asks for the future time slots. Trading is enabled at future time slots $t +1, \dots, t + 24$ at current time slot t. The retail market allows brokers to build their customer portfolio by means of offering multiple tariffs to local producers and consumers. In the middle of the retail and wholesale markets, the distribution utility keeps track of supply and demand, and charges brokers for their imbalanced energy. Customers are simulated as independent consumer and producer models such as electric vehicles, house-holds, storage units and solar panels. The interaction between customers and brokers takes place in the retail market through tariff subscriptions.

---

[1] The row indicates wholesale costs without taxes, profits and service fees.

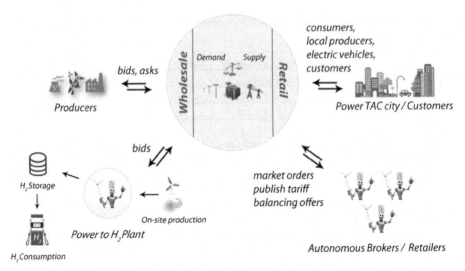

Fig. 1. Simulation model in Power TAC scenario.

Table 3. Parameters of the proposed ecosystem.

	Symbol	Description	Value
Size of electrolysis unit	S^{elc}	Size of unit which converts electricity to H_2.	10 MW
Size of H_2 storage unit	S^{str}	Size of storage unit in which produced H_2 is stored.	1000 kg
Electrolyser efficiency vector	E^{elc}	Efficiency vector of an electrolysis unit based on the rate of (electricity input/ S^{elc}).	[0 – 85 %]
Energy equiv. of 1 MWh electricity	R^{ptg}	Equivalence of 1 MWh electrical power to H_2 regardless of losses.	30 kg H_2
Learning alpha	Q_ALPHA	Alpha parameter of Q-learning.	0.5
Learning gamma	Q_GAMMA	Gamma parameter of Q-learning	0.0
Time horizon	H	Total length of a game in time slot.	8765
Future time slot	T	Future time slots which are enabled for trading.	24
Bidding margin	M	Margin that is added to the price obtain through MDP.	5 EUR

The proposed refilling station simulates the following components:

— Electrolysis Unit: Converts input power to hydrogen having an efficiency rate which depends on the size of electrolysis unit and input power.
— Hydrogen Storage Unit: This unit stores the produced hydrogen thorough electrolysis process. It also supplies hydrogen to dispensers.
— Dispensers: Final end-point where refilling hydrogen to simulated fuel cell vehicles takes place.
— A number of fuel cell and traditional vehicles.

— On-site solar panels and wind mills which supply electricity to electrolysis unit.
— Trader module: Trades in the wholesale market and optimize the costs considering various variables and on-site production.

Trading in the wholesale market is the most significant part of the research since the motivation of the research is to benefit from the excess energy. Unlike electricity retailers, hydrogen trader unit can make flexible decisions and watch cheap prices at future hours thanks to its hydrogen storage unit. Storage unit can easily tolerate several time slots to let trader unit find cheaper energy in an hour-ahead market.

3.1   Trading Model

Unlike broker models in the ecosystem, power-to-gas models are supposed to have an appropriate trading model. Brokers have to deal with balancing problems and make careful decisions to avoid balancing penalties. In order to meet supply and demand, brokers might submit extremely generous bids. However, this landscape is a bit different for power-to-gas plants. Thanks to their storage units, they are able to make more flexible decisions. Following statement presents the optimization problem of overall cost over time horizon H.

$$min \sum_{t=1}^{H} \sum_{n=1}^{T} e_n^t \cdot p_n^t \tag{1}$$

Where e is energy and p is energy price over time horizon H and enable future time slots T. In order to optimize the wholesale market cost over a time horizon, we propose a trading model using Markov Decision Process (MDP) design, deploying a Q-learning method [17]. In this approach, all hours are represented as 24 individual processes. Each process has 25 states which represent the future time slot proximity as well as *completed* state. Proposed MDP is designed as follows:

— **States:** $s \in \{1, ..., 24, completed\}$
— **Terminal state:** $\{completed\}$
— **Reward function:** In state $\{completed\}$, the reward function returns 0. Otherwise, it returns 0.
— **Actions:** $limitPrice_s \in \mathbb{Z} : s = 24$, $limitPrice_s - clearingPrice_{s+1} \in \mathbb{Z} : s < 24$.
— **Transition function:** In a state $s \in \{1, ..., 24\}$, if an order fully clears, it transitions to *completed* state. Otherwise, s transitions to s-1.   In every time slot, a new episode starts for processes where s = 0.

In this MDP design, actions are defined as difference of limit price and clearing price which cleared in previous state. In other words, actions indicate increment values as state s transitions to s - 1. This way provides many opportunities such as catching price trends regardless of weather conditions. Even if a bid does not clear at s = 24, next bids eventually become more adaptive.

In the learning mode, delayed market data is used to update Q-matrix. Therefore, actions are defined as $clearingPrice_s \in \mathbb{Z} : s = 24$, $clearingPrice_s - clearingPrice_{s+1} \in \mathbb{Z} : s < 24$. Following Q-learning formula evaluates the market experience of the agent.

$$Q_{t+1}(s_t, a_t) = Q_t(s_t, a_t) * \alpha + (R_{t+1} + \ * \ max_a \ Q_t(s_{t+1}, a_t)) * (1 - \alpha) \qquad (2)$$

Subject to $0 \leq \alpha \leq 1$ and $0 \leq \gamma \leq 1$. After each iteration, Q matrix is normalized to make sure that all values are set between 1 and 0.

Solving MDP is straight forward since it only requires searching the right value in the state-action vector. Following formula fetches the predicted price at current time slot t and future time slot T.

$$MDP(t, T) = clearingPrice_{t-1, T} + (arg \ max_a \ Q_t(T - t, a_t)) \qquad (3)$$

However, various trading approaches are required to optimize the overall cost. Using predicted prices through MDP's might be helpful to find the future prices. But another procedure is needed to catch cheap prices and skip expensive wholesale prices. To achieve this, we propose 4 trading approaches defined as follows.

- **Stingy:** This bidding approach always submit lower prices than solved prices through MDP. Submitted price will be *solveMDP(t, T)* - M where M is set to 5.
- **Neutral:** Solved price through MDP is directly submitted in the order.
- **Generous:** Unlike Stingy approach, it always submit generous prices than solved prices through MDP. Final price will be *solveMDP(t, T)* + M where M is set to 5.
- **Combined:** This strategy combines all of the approaches above. For a particular current time slot *t*, predicted prices (for future time slot *T*) at *t, t + 1, ... , T − 1* are divided into 3 price zones which are defined as cheap, normal and expensive. In cheap zone, generous bidding is used to increase the chance of buying cheap energy. In normal price zone, neutral bidding strategy is used. Likewise, stingy bidding is used in expensive price zone to decrease the probability of buying expensive energy.

As a future work, these strategies will be integrated to hydrogen storage optimization problem to minimize overall cost of refilling station.

4   Future Work

Proposed design above enables various studies from different perspectives. First, a legal landscape (taxation, incentives and transition policies) and a future projection will be covered under this research. Second, renewables have to be taken into account deeply since they are the main drivers of the future energy production. Within this scope, all of penetration levels will be simulated with the proposed trading methods. Third, size of refilling station, such size of electrolysis unit, storage unit, pumps and so on, will be subject to an optimization problem considering investment and operational costs.

This work aims to control a number of variables.

- Size of electrolysis unit (MW). An electrolysis unit is the most efficient at 25% electricity input.

- Size of hydrogen storage (kg). A bigger size of storage unit can put trader unit into a more flexible position. Therefore, operating modes will be defined based on the hydrogen storage.
- Share of vehicle groups. Percentages of fuel cells, battery electric vehicles and traditional vehicles among all passenger vehicles (cars, buses, vans).
- Production volume (including local producers). Various production rates will be subject to experiments.
- Distribution fee. This fee is paid if the bought energy is originated from wholesale market. Incentives can waive this fee.
- Trading approaches. These approaches will be defined in Markov processes later on.
- Number of retailer/broker companies.

All of these variables are controlled to optimize the cost and investment problems as well as further possible analysis. Existing works in the literature are usually based on the static data or estimations. Power-to-gas is usually considered as a profitability problem or balancing approach which are far away from transportation perspective.

5 Conclusion

In summary, the smart grid will bring a lot of benefits such as excess energy. On the other side, fuel cells have all the functionalities of a battery electric vehicle in addition to hydrogen storage and fuel cell stack. This capability provides opportunity to drive with hydrogen or electricity no matter which one is available in the vehicle. Obviously, both ways are nature friendly and do not replace each other.

Proposed trading approaches and design show that power-to-hydrogen units are able to trade in the wholesale markets, making more flexible decisions thank to hydrogen storage units. It is noteworthy that unstable energy production by renewables eventually results in unstable price regime. This highly volatile environment will be the driver of power-to-gas plants.

References

1. Hall, P., Bain, P.: Energy-storage technologies and electricity generation. Elsevier (2008)
2. Mineralölwirtschaftsverbande, V.: Statistiken–Preise. December 3, 2014. http://www.mwv. de/index.php/daten/statistikenpreise/?loc=1
3. Pure Energy Centre. Hydrogen refueling station. December 5, 2014. http://pureenergycentre. com/hydrogen-fueling-station/
4. Kurier. ErsteWasserstoff-Tankstelle: Künftigtankenwir Kilos. December 12, 2014. http:// kurier.at/wirtschaft/1-wasserstoff-tankstelle-kuenftig-tanken-wir-kilos/824.355
5. Verivox. Direktvergleich. November 24, 2014. http://www.verivox.de/strompreisvergleich
6. Clever Tanken. Aktuelle Diesel, Benzinpreise. December 11, 2014. http://www.clever-tanken.de
7. Nord Pool Spot. Nordic and Baltic Trading Fees. December 11, 2014. http://www. nordpoolspot.com/TAS/Fees/Nordic-Baltic/

8. EPEX Spot. Price List. December 14, 2014. http://static.epexspot.com/document/29089/EPEXSPOT_Price_List_January_2015.pdf
9. Federal Ministry of Transport and Digital Infrastructure (BMVI). Power-to-Gas (PtG) in transport: Status quo and perspectives for development. Berlin (2014)
10. National Renewable Energy Laboratory. Hydrogen Station Compression, Storage, and Dispensing Technical Status and Costs (2014)
11. Zero Regio. The future cost and competitiveness of hydrogen as a transport fuel in Europe (2010)
12. Lizbeth, C.G.M.: Assessment of usage of hydrogen as alternative fuel into NETPLAN (PhD dissertation). Iowa State University (2013)
13. Fuel Cell Today. Water Electrolysis & Renewable Energy Systems (2013)
14. Sterner, M.: Power-to-Gas: PerspektiveneinerjungenTechnologie (2013)
15. Reichert, F., Brian, V.M.: Wind-to-Gas-to-Money? Economics and Perspectives of the Power-to-Gas Technology (master thesis). Aalborg University (2012)
16. Ketter, W., Collins, J., Reddy, P.P., Weerdt, M.D.: The 2015 Power Trading Agent Competition. ERIM Report Series Reference No. ERS-2015-001-LIS (2015)
17. Watkins, C.J., Dayan, P.: Q-learning. Machine learning **8**(3–4), 279–292 (1992)

Computational Intelligence
and Algorithms

Computational Intelligence Approach to Capturing the Implied Volatility

Fahed Mostafa[1], Tharam Dillon[1(✉)], and Elizabeth Chang[2]

[1] Deptartment of Computer Science and IT, La Trobe University, Melbourne, Australia
fahedm@yahoo.com, Tharam.dillon7@gmail.com
[2] School of Business, ADFA and UNSW at Canberra, Canberra, Australia
E.Chang@adfa.edu.au

Abstract. In this paper, a Computational Intelligence Approach and more particularly a neural network is used to learn from data on the Black-Scholes implied volatility. The implied volatility forecasts, generated from the Neural Net, are converted to option price using the Black-Scholes formula. The neural network option pricing capabilities are shown to be superior to the Black-Scholes and the GARCH option-pricing model. The neural network has also shown that it is able to reproduce the implied volatility well into the future whereas the GARCH option-pricing model shows deterioration in the implied volatility with time.

Keywords: Computational intelligence · Neural networks · Option pricing · Implied volatility · GARCH option pricing model

1 Introduction

The Black-Scholes Option Pricing Model (BSOPM) published in 1973 (Black and Scholes 1973) remains one of the most cited scientific papers in this field. The model made a key contribution to option trading, allowing investors to calculate a fair value for an option contract. This model has its limitations, which stem from the unrealistic assumptions used in the derivation of the BSOPM. The wide success of this model was due to its ability to produce an option price instantaneously. The formulation of BSOPM was based on major assumptions which allowed for the derivation of this model. These assumptions significantly impacted the model pricing capabilities which are visible in the models pricing biases. The constant volatility assumption has captured the attention of researchers, as it contradicts the volatility behaviour observed in the underlying asset. Also, it was realised when the volatility was backed out from the BSOPM for different strike prices, the implied volatility displays a U-shape pattern (volatility smile) when plotted against the options moneyness. Moneyness is defined as the relative position of the current or future price of the underlying asset with respect to the option strike price. Nevertheless, implied volatility is derived directly from the options data, which contains vital information as it provides a forward looking view on how the market is anticipating movements in the underlying asset. This is a different view to the conditional volatility calculated from the stock returns which is

© IFIP International Federation for Information Processing 2015
T. Dillon (Ed.): IFIP AI 2015, IFIP AICT 465, pp. 85–97, 2015.
DOI: 10.1007/978-3-319-25261-2_8

a retrospective view. The other interesting feature of the implied volatility is the deterioration of the volatility surface through time caused by the changes in the implied volatility levels. Many models have emerged to overcome the limitations of the BSOPM. In the present paper, we select the GARCH option pricing model (GOPM hereafter) as it allows for the volatility to follow a GARCH specification. This specification overcomes the constant volatility assumptions and at the same time caters for key stylised facts in the underlying returns series. This model has displayed superior improvements over other pricing models. The major shortcoming for this model is the absence of a closed form solution. This means the model parameters have to be optimised using a Monte Carlo simulation, which is a computationally intensive process that limits its ability to be applied to real-life problems.

Neural networks have been applied previously to option pricing problems (Karaali, Edelberg et al. 1997), (Meissner and Kawano 2001), (Amilon 2003), (Yao, Li et al. 2000), (Tino, Schittenkopf et al. 2001) and (Bennell and Sutcliffe 2004). The majority of research papers rely on neural networks to provide a mapping from inputs similar to the BSOPM to the option price. Training the neural network on the option price is a cumbersome task. The option itself can suffer from many issues such as stale prices due to infrequent trading (Rubinstein 1985). Therefore, using the option price to guide the training of the neural network can be misleading as the neural network will attempt to map the inputs to an output that has poor correlation with the input. To overcome this limitation, many variations of this method have been developed to improve the pricing accuracy. For instance, substantial pricing performance gains are achieved when the training data set is partitioned by moneyness and different neural networks are used for each of the training sets. Yet there has been no attempt to evaluate the neural networks' performance against more advanced models. The reason for this is that the pricing capabilities of the neural networks are inferior to those of more advanced pricing models such as the GOPM. In (Hanke 1997), a neural network was constructed to give an approximate price to GOPM. This was achieved by training the network on different input combinations for the GOPM allowing the neural networks to approximate the GOPM, thereby overcoming the numerical simulation issues of the GOPM. In (Mostafa and Dillon 2008), a new option pricing method was proposed by allowing the neural network to learn the implied volatility behaviour of the option through time.

The main variable that can explain the option behaviour through time is the implied volatility, since the implied volatility is considered to be a forward looking view of the market anticipation. By allowing the neural network to capture the implied volatility surface through time, the neural network will be able to forecast future movements of the implied volatility across different strikes which can then be converted to an option price. This method was demonstrated to have superior option pricing over the Black-Scholes and GOPM. The option pricing of the neural network and GOPM was discussed and analysed in (Mostafa and Dillon 2008), in this paper we demonstrate the capabilities of neural networks in learning the implied volatility surface through time and its impact on option pricing. We also validate this method by studying how well the neural network can reproduce implied volatility into the future relative to the GOPM. In section 2, the option pricing models are reviewed; in section 3 the data used in this paper is explained. In section 4 the performance measuring criteria are explained, in section 5 the results from the experiments are discussed. In section 6 we discuss and compare the implied volatility forecast behaviour of the neural network and GOPM. We then conclude this paper in section 7.

2   Option Pricing Models

In this section we review the option pricing models studied in this paper.

2.1   GARCH Option Pricing Model (GOPM)

It has been demonstrated by (Duan 1995) that under the Local Risk Neutral Valuation Relationship (LRNVR) the conditional variance does not change. However, under measure Q , the conditional expectation of rt is the risk free rate r_f.

$$E^Q\left[\exp(r_t) \mid \Omega_{t-1}\right] = \exp(r_f) \tag{1}$$

To derive the GOPM, the risk neutral valuation relationship has to be generalized to the LRNVR:

$$r_t = r_f - \frac{1}{2}\sigma_t^{*2} + \sigma_t^* \varepsilon_t^*, where \ \varepsilon_t^* \sim N(0,1) \tag{2}$$

$$\sigma_t^{*2} = \beta_0 + \beta_1(\varepsilon_{t-1}^* - \tilde{\gamma})^2 \sigma_{t-1}^{*2} + \beta_2 \sigma_{t-1}^{*2} \tag{3}$$

By having $\tilde{\gamma} = \lambda + \gamma$, the risk-neutral pricing measure is determined by four parameters: $\beta_0, \beta_1, \beta_2$ and $\tilde{\gamma}$. Using the above formulation, the asset terminal is then calculated at time T

$$S_T = S_t \exp\left(r_f(T-t) - \frac{1}{2}\sum_{i=t+1}^{T}\sigma_i^{*2} + \sum_{i=t+1}^{T}\sigma_i^*\varepsilon_i^*\right) \tag{4}$$

The terminal asset price is then calculated using Monte Carlo simulation. A set of N random path of residuals $(\varepsilon_{t+1,j}^*,...,\varepsilon_{T,j}^*)$ is generated with J = 1 to N. The residuals are used to calculate the asset prices $S_{T,j}$. The final option price is then approximated as follows:

$$C_{GARCH} = \exp(-r_f^*(T-t))\frac{1}{N}\sum_{j=1}^{M}\max(S_{T,j} - K, 0) \tag{5}$$

Empirical Martingale Simulation (EMS) of (Duan and Simonato 1998) has been used which has been shown to accelerate the convergence of the Monte Carlo prices estimates. The GOPM parameters were estimated for each day of the data sample. This was achieved by minimizing the average sum squared error eqn. (21) (Aboura 2005) (Lehnert) over all options on day t, with parameters from day t-1 as the initial values (Lehar, Scheicher et al. 2002).

$$\text{Min } SSE\ (\Theta) = \sum_{t=1}^{T} \sum_{n=1}^{N} \left| \frac{\left(\hat{C}_{t,n} - C_{t,n} \right)}{C_{t,n}} \right| \tag{6}$$

where $\Theta = \{\beta_0, \beta_1, \beta_2, \lambda\}$, $\hat{C}$ and C are the model theoretical price and the actual call price respectively. The number of Monte Carlo simulations was initially set to 15,000. This was sufficient to generate stable estimates. In some cases, the number of simulations had to be increased to 30,000.

2.2   The Black-Scholes Option Pricing Model (BSOPM)

The BSOPM theorem was first published in 1971 (Black and Scholes 1973). It is the most widely used pricing model. The interest rate and volatility are constant; the call option on the asset, expiring at time T and with strike price K will have the following value at time t:

$$C(t,T) = S(t)N(d_1) - Ke^{-r(T-t)}N(d_2) \tag{7}$$

where, $d_1 = \dfrac{\ln\left(\dfrac{S(t)}{K}\right) + \left(r + \dfrac{\sigma^2}{2}\right)(T-t)}{\sigma\sqrt{T-t}}$ and $d_2 = \dfrac{\ln\left(\dfrac{S(t)}{K}\right) + \left(r - \dfrac{\sigma^2}{2}\right)(T-t)}{\sigma\sqrt{T-t}}$

$N(x)$ is the cumulative probability distribution for a standard normally distributed variable. The BSOPM delta is given by $N(d_1)$, which also measures the sensitivity to the underlying asset.

2.2.1 Implied Volatility
The implied volatility is a volatility parameter, which equates the market price with the price given by the BSOPM formula. The implied volatility, $\sigma_t^{BS}(K,T)$ is a function of K (Strike) and T (time to maturity) (Hull 2003). The two most interesting features of the volatility surface, which have been studied and analysed by researchers, are the volatility smile (skew) and the term structure or the level of implied volatility changes with time. The volatility smile is a key indicator of an unrealistic assumption of constant volatility. Whereas, the changes in the implied volatility level with time is seen by the deformation of the volatility surface with time. Therefore, the ability to capture the implied volatility term structure will lead to accurate option pricing. (Cont and da Fonseca 2001) have expressed mathematically the implied volatility surface as follows:

$$C_{BS}\left(S_t, K, \tau, \sigma_t^{BS}(K,T)\right) = C_t^*(K,T), \text{ where } \sigma_t^{BS}(K,T) > 0 \tag{8}$$

The value of the call option as a function of the volatility is a monotonic mapping from $[0,+\infty[$ to $]0, S_t\text{-}Ke^{-rt}[$. The implied volatility $\sigma_t^{BS}(K,T)$ of a call option with strike K and price maturity of T is dependent on K and T. If K and T are fixed, $\sigma_t^{BS}(K,T)$ can be generalised to follow a stochastic process. For a fixed t, the value will depend on the options characteristics such as maturity and strike level K. Equation 9 represents the volatility surface at time t.

$$\sigma_t^{BS} : (K,T) \longrightarrow \sigma_t^{BS}(K,T) \tag{9}$$

$$I_t(m,\tau) = \sigma_t^{BS}(mS(t), t+\tau) \tag{10}$$

Where m is the moneyness, $I_t(m,\tau)$ is the implied volatility function.

The two most important features of this surface are the volatility smile and the changes in the volatility levels with time. Thus, the evolution in time of this surface will reflect the evolution of market option prices. Many previous studies have attempted to explain the information contained in the implied volatility (Day and Lewis 1992; Canina and Figlewski 1993; Christensen and Prabhala 1998; Blair, Poon et al. 2001; Jiang and Tian 2005) where the majority of studies have shown that the implied volatilities contain relevant measurement errors with quantifiable magnitude. Earlier research shows the implied volatility to be an inefficient forecast of volatility (Canina and Figlewski 1993). However, more recent studies such as (Jiang and Tian 2005) show that the implied volatility subsumes all information contained in the historical volatility and is capable of providing an accurate forecast of future volatility. This information can be utilised in many aspects since the option prices reflect the participant's expectations of the market's future movements. So, if the option market is efficient such that all information is observed and the correct option pricing model is specified, the implied volatility should subsume the information contained in other variables in explaining future volatility. That is, the implied volatility should be an efficient forecast of future trends over the life of the option.

There have been several theoretical explanations for the volatility smile such as the distribution assumption and stochastic volatility (Poon 2005). There have been other explanations proposed based on market microstructure, measurement errors and investor risk preference. However, the BSOPM assumes the asset price to have a lognormal distribution or the (logarithmic) returns to follow a normal distribution. Given a high strike price the call option is deep out-of-the-money and the option has a very low probability that it will be exercised. The leptokurtic right tail will give the option a higher probability than the normal distribution for the asset price to exceed the strike price, which means the call will be in-the-money at expiry. If we consider a low strike price, the same argument applies as above but an out-of-the-money put option is used instead. Due to the thicker left tail of the leptokurtic distribution, the probability of the out-of-the-money put option to finish in-the-money will be higher than that of the normal distribution. Therefore, the put option price should be greater than the price given by the BSOPM. If the BSOPM is used to back out the implied volatility, the BSOPM implied volatility will be higher than the actual volatility. This causes the volatility smile where the implied volatility is much higher at very low strike prices and low at high strike prices. The implied volatility for different strikes and maturities do not evolve independently and they are a highly correlated multivariate system (Cont and Fonseca 2002). To construct a model in terms of the implied volatility rather than volatility of the underlying asset volatility may complicate the modelling procedure. However, there are advantages of modelling the implied volatility directly. For instance, the implied volatility is observable and is derived from the market data, whereas, the asset volatility is not directly observable. The implied volatility gives an insight to the option markets which can be analysed by the practitioners. The shifts in levels of implied volatility are highly correlated across strikes and maturities, which allows for the modelling of the joint dynamics. The implied volatility is now widely used by practitioners and especially with the emergence of implied volatility indexes and derivative instruments (Cont and Fonseca 2002).

2.3 Artificial Neural Network (ANN)

The ANN consists mainly of an input layer, one more hidden layer and an output layer. The layers are connected via a set of weights. The hidden layer and the output layer consist of individual neurons. The inputs are multiplied by the weights and a bias term is added which then constitutes the input to the activation function. This then serves as the input to the following layer. The activation of the output layer is given by:

$$F(x) = G(\sum_J w_{ij} H(\sum_K w_{jk} x_k + B_k) + B_J) \tag{11}$$

The activation functions of the neurons could be chosen to be linear or non-linear functions. A sum of error-squared function is normally used as the objective function for the training of the MLP. So the MLP is trained to minimize this function with respect to the in-sample data.

$$E = \frac{1}{N} \sum_1^N (t_i - F_i(x))^2 \tag{12}$$

The MLP performance is dependent on the initial values of the weights. To overcome this issue, the neural network is trained 50 times using different initial values for the weights. The weight set that introduces the least error is then adopted.

Given the limited success in applying neural networks to option pricing, we adopt the same method used in (Mostafa and Dillon 2008) for training the neural network with the intention of capturing the underlying asset dynamics of the instrument which then can be translated to an option price using known market variables. This new methodology allows the neural network to capture the dynamics of the underlying asset and the changes in the volatility levels through time. Using the option price to train the neural network has been proven to be ineffective; therefore, instead of training the neural network to price the option directly, we allow the neural network to learn the implied volatility. So the neural network will be optimized on the implied volatility, thereby allowing the neural network to forecast the implied volatility for different maturities and moneyness. Many studies have demonstrated that vital information is contained in the implied volatility especially since the implied volatility contains the market expectation of the underlying asset future movements. To allow the neural network to capture the entire volatility surface, the data set was not partitioned by moneyness, thereby allowing the neural network full visibility of the volatility surface. This approach is a mapping exercise described in equation 14. The neural networks must be tested and verified on the training data set to overcome key issues such as over-fitting (Mostafa and Dillon 2008). The neural network is trained using the BSOPM implied volatility as the target output. This method allows the neural network to predict the future implied volatility, which also means that the neural network can produce the implied volatility surface over any trading horizon. The implied volatility can be converted to an option price by plugging it into the BSOPM. The neural networks were optimized by varying the number of inputs, length of in-sample and validation sets, and the number of hidden units. The combination that gives the lowest error is considered to be the optimal model and is chosen accordingly. The initial weight values were initialized randomly, and to eliminate the dependency on the initial weight values, this process was repeated 50 times.

After experimentation with the different inputs, the following combination was selected for optimal performance. The in-sample and validation set were 20 and 5 days respectively, and the output sample was 1 day. The inputs used were moneyness (index/strike), time to expiry and historical volatility. The target data set was the BSOPM implied volatility. Once the training of the ANN is completed, the implied volatility produced by the ANN would be plugged into the Black-Scholes formula to obtain an analytical price of the option. This model would be referred to as NNiv.

3   Data

The data used in this research consists of European call options on the FTSE 100 index traded at the London International Financial and Options Exchange (LIFFE). The data for this research was obtained from SIRCA (http://www.sirca.org.au/), which covered a two-year period starting from 2/1/2000 and ending on 31/12/2001. The sample was made up of 63,094 call options and the daily Index value (adjusted for dividends). The following constraints were applied to filter the data series: moneyness (index/strike) outside [-1.01,0.9], maturity greater 175 days and less than 7 days and close price less than five where removed. The data series was then reduced to 26533 options. GB Libor rates were used for the risk-free rate inputs to the models. The parameters for the GOPM and BSOPM were estimated on a daily basis. However, when optimising the ANN, the data was split into 3 sets: in-sample, validation and out-of-sample. The in-sample set is used as input to the ANN, thus impacting on the weights. The validation set is used to evaluate the error at each epoch. The training of the network is terminated when the error of the validation increases. The out-of-sample data set is used for evaluating the ANN model.

4   Performance Measure

To analyze the model's performance, Absolute Relative Pricing Error (ARPE) was calculated for each model. where $\hat{C}$ and C is the model theoretical call price and the actual call price. The errors are reported against maturity and moneyness. The models pricing performance is further analyzed by running a regression analysis to study the pricing behavior based on the moneyness and TTE (Time to Expiry).

$$ARPE = \frac{1}{n}\sum_{i=1}^{n}\left|\frac{\hat{C}_i - C_i}{C_i}\right| \tag{13}$$

$$ARPE = aTTE + bMon + c + \varepsilon \text{ , where } \varepsilon \sim N(0,\sigma^2) \tag{14}$$

5   Results

Below the estimated mean values of the GOPM parameters are given in Table 1.

Table 1. GOPM average parameters

β_0	β_1	β_2	γ	$\sqrt{\sigma}$
3.109E-05	1.848E-01	3.184E-01	6.745E-01	22.37%

The risk premium is extracted from the option prices rather than from the index time series. It was found to be a little weak which in turn will have a minor impact on the option price. The annual volatility was found to be approx 22.37% which is a close approximation to the historical vol atility when estimated on the index prices 20.7%.

The ARPE figures are displayed in Table 2. On average, the performances of GOPM and NNiv models increase with maturity. Again, the BSOPM performs the worst on all accounts. On average, the NNiv has a slightly better performance than the GOPM. The GOPM model performs slightly better for MT contracts and the NNiv has a better performance for ST and LT contracts. All models have performed the worst for ST-DOTM contracts. In addition, the GOPM performs the best for LT-DITM, whereas the NNiv and BSOPM are at their best for ST-DITM contracts. The NNiv seems to perform best for the MT-ITM contracts. The ARPE is regressed on TTE (Time to Expiry) and Mon (Moneyness). The estimated coefficients are displayed in Table 3. The coefficients R^2 and *F-test* for NNiv and the GOPM are similar. This indicates that the models price the options in a similar manner. For all models, the ARPE is smaller for longer maturities and increased moneyness. Therefore, ITM options are priced more accurately than the OTM options and the models price LT contracts with better accuracy than ST contracts.

6   The Empirical Dynamics of the Volatility Smile

In this section, we study the behavior of the implied volatility of the GOPM and the NNiv over time. The implied volatility of NNiv is given directly as the output of the model, whereas the GOPM produces a theoretical option price. To extract the implied volatility from the GOPM, the option prices are equated to the BSOPM formula and the implied volatility is backed out. To study the volatility smile, a theoretical series is generated by an out-of-sample fit of the GOPM parameters calculated on the previous day. The implied volatility is then backed out for each option price using the BSOPM formula. Figure 1 shows the first day out-of-sample forecast for the GOPM. It can be seen that the volatilities are higher for the shorter maturities. As the option moves from ITM to ATM, they converge and the slopes are reversed.

Table 2. ARPE for all models against the options time to maturity.

Moneyness	Model	Time to Maturity			
		LT (Long TTE)	MT (Medium TTE)	ST (Short TTE)	TOTAL
DOTM (Deep Out of the money)	GOPM	0.179	0.246	0.384	0.267
	BSOPM	0.993	1.815	1.289	1.584
	NNiv	0.167	0.269	0.358	0.273
OTM (Out of The Money)	GOPM	0.105	0.157	0.272	0.202
	BSOPM	0.502	0.713	0.984	0.809
	NNiv	0.102	0.154	0.262	0.195
ATM (At the money)	GOPM	0.078	0.1	0.139	0.116
	BSOPM	0.274	0.262	0.277	0.27
	NNiv	0.086	0.094	0.135	0.112
ITM (In The Money)	GOPM	0.082	0.074	0.079	0.077
	BSOPM	0.169	0.12	0.077	0.104
	NNiv	0.081	0.071	0.075	0.074
DITM (Deep In The Money)	GOPM	0.039	0.061	0.05	0.053
	BSOPM	0.099	0.074	0.051	0.069
	NNiv	0.098	0.066	0.058	0.068
All	GOPM	0.121	0.167	0.233	0.188
	BSOPM	0.589	0.924	0.742	0.818
	NNiv	0.119	0.172	0.222	0.185

This has been highlighted by (Aboura 2005), where this point is of importance because the model is able to classify the volatilities according to their moneyness. Figure 2 displays the implied volatility for the end of the month using the same parameters as those for the first day of the month. The deformation of the smiles is obvious. The short maturity has a higher implied volatility; however, the skew of the longer maturities becomes more linear.

The theoretical volatilities calculated for NNiv at the first day of the month are displayed in Figure 3. The volatility smile is apparent in the graph. The graph also shows a similar behavior to the skews generated by the GOPM. For all maturities, the slope of the skews changes as it moves from ITM to OTM. So, as the option approaches ATM, the volatilities across all maturities become similar. For the ITM - LT option, the skew tends to be linear; then as it moves past the ATM point, the NN gives higher volatilities. For ITM-ST options, the NN generates much larger volatilities than the ITM-LT options. As ST option passes the ATM range, the slope changes direction forming the smile. However, the volatilities are smaller than the LT for OTM options.

Table 3. Regression results

	NNiv	GOPM	BSOPM
C	2.097	2.052	13.931
	(-46.116)	*(-45.072)*	*(69.214)*
A	-0.327	-0.330	-0.769
	(-26.065)	*(-26.306)*	*(-13.869)*
B	-1.900	-1.851	-13.372
	(-40.983)	*(-39.865)*	*(-65.148)*
R²	14.66%	13.71%	25.05%
F-test	1047.439	1014.297	2133.957

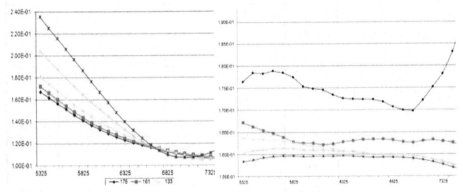

Fig. 1. GOPM out-of-sample skews for 4/9/2000

Fig. 2. GOPM out-of-sample skews for 28/9/2000

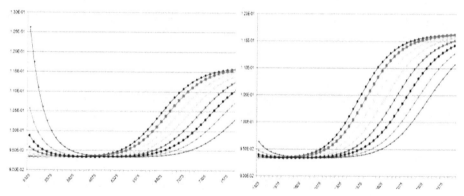

Fig. 3. NNiv out of sample skews for 4/9/2000

Fig. 4. NNiv out of sample skews for 28/9/2000

In Figure 4, there does not seem to be any deformation of the skews. The skews also follow the same behavior as those in Figure 3. The deformation of the GOPM skews through time displays that the model is sensitive to changes in the underlying asset. The GOPM parameters are calibrated under LRNVR conditions by simulating the underlying asset process and pricing the options at expiry accordingly. However, the NNiv is designed and trained differently. The ability of the NNiv to price options out-of-sample is a key indicator of the ability of the NN to capture the dynamics of the options. The NNiv trained on mapping the input space (TTE, Moneyness, Historical Volatility) to Black-Scholes implied volatility. Due to the high number of variables in the NN, 1 day of historical data was not sufficient to produce a stable result. Hence, the NN was trained on 20 days of data, which contains substantial information. Therefore, when the smiles are generated out-of-sample towards the expiry of the options, the neural network is able to display the actual skew at that point in time. This is a good indication that the NN is a suitable tool for long-term forecasting.

7   Conclusion

The neural network was trained using the implied volatility as the target output of the neural network rather than the options price. This method has shown to have superior out-of-sample pricing performance over the BSOPM and GOPM. The neural network's performance was also compared to those of the GOPM and the BSOPM. The regression analysis shows the neural network behaves in a similar manner to the GOPM. This demonstrates the neural networks are capable of learning and reproducing option prices accurately by learning the implied volatility. The neural network was also shown to reproduce the implied volatility well into the future where as the GOPM start to show deformation. This behavior of the neural network demonstrates its capabilities to capture the underlying asset volatility structure and volatility levels through time. This can contain vital information on future market behaviors. In future research, this method will be further expanded and applied to Value-at-Risk models.

References

Aboura, S.: GARCH Option Pricing Under Skew. Journal: The ICFAI Journal of Applied Economics 4(6), 78–86 (2005)

Amilon, H.: A neural network versus Black-Scholes: a comparison of pricing and hedging performances. Journal of Forecasting 22(4), 317–335 (2003)

Bennell, J., Sutcliffe, C.: Black-Scholes versus artificial neural networks in pricing FTSE 100 options. Intelligent Systems in Accounting, Finance & Management 12(4), 243–260 (2004)

Black, F., Scholes, M.: The Pricing of Options and Corporate Liabilities. The Journal of Political Economy 81(3), 637–654 (1973)

Blair, B.J., Poon, S.H., et al.: Forecasting S&P 100 volatility: the incremental information content of implied volatilities and high-frequency index returns. Journal of Econometrics 105(1), 5–26 (2001)

Canina, L., Figlewski, S.: The informational content of implied volatility. Review of Financial Studies 6(3), 659 (1993)

Christensen, B.J., Prabhala, N.R.: The relation between implied and realized volatility1. Journal of Financial Economics 50(2), 125–150 (1998)

Cont, R., da Fonseca, J.: Deformation of implied volatility surfaces: an empirical analysis. In: Empirical Approaches to Financial Fluctuations (2001)

Cont, R., Fonseca, J.: Dynamics of implied volatility surfaces. Quantitative Finance 2(1), 45–60 (2002)

Day, T.E., Lewis, C.M.: Stock Market Volatility and the Informational Content of Stock Index Options. Journal of Econometrics 52(1) (1992)

Duan, J.C.: The GARCH Option Pricing Model. Mathematical Finance 5(1), 13–32 (1995)

Duan, J.C., Simonato, J.G.: Empirical Martingale Simulation for Asset Prices. Management Science 44(9), 1218–1233 (1998)

Dumas, B., Fleming, J., et al.: Implied volatility functions: Empirical tests. Journal of Finance 53(6), 2059–2106 (1998)

Hanke, M.: Neural Network Approximation of Option Pricing Formulas for Analytically Intractable Option Pricing Models. Journal of Computational Intelligence in Finance 5(5), 20–27 (1997)

Hull, J.: Options, futures, and other derivatives. Prentice Hall Upper Saddle River, NJ (2003)

Jiang, G.J., Tian, Y.S.: The model-free implied volatility and its information content. Review of Financial Studies 18(4), 1305 (2005)

Karaali, O., Edelberg, W., et al.: Modelling volatility derivatives using neural networks. In: Proceedings of the IEEE/IAFE 1997 Computational Intelligence for Financial Engineering (CIFEr), pp. 280–286 (1997)

Lehar, A., Scheicher, M., et al.: GARCH vs. stochastic volatility: Option pricing and risk management. Journal of Banking and Finance 26(2–3), 323–345 (2002)

Lehnert, T.: Mandelbrot and the Smile

Meissner, G., Kawano, N.: Capturing the Volatility Smile of Options on High-Tech Stocks-A Combined GARCH-Neural Network Approach. Journal of Economics and Finance 25(3), 276–292 (2001)

Mostafa, F., Dillon, T.: Modelling volatility with mixture density networks. In: IEEE International Conference on Granular Computing, GrC 2008 (2008)

Mostafa, F., Dillon, T.: A neural network approach to option pricing. Computational Finance and its Applications III (2008)

Poon, S.H.: A practical Guide to Forecasting Financial Market Volatility. Wiley, New York (2005)

Rubinstein, M.: Nonparametric tests of alternative option pricing models using all reported trades and quotes on the 30 most active CBOE option classes from August 23, 1976 through August 31, 1978. The Journal of Finance **40**(2), 455–480 (1985)

Tino, P., Schittenkopf, C., et al.: Financial volatility trading using recurrent neural networks. IEEE Transactions on Neural Networks **12**(4), 865–874 (2001)

Yao, J., Li, Y., et al.: Option price forecasting using neural networks. Omega **28**(4), 455–466 (2000)

CCF-Based Awareness in Agent Model ABGP

Zhongzhi Shi[1](✉), Jinpeng Yue[1,2], Gang Ma[1,2], and Xi Yang[1]

[1] Key Laboratory of Intelligent Information Processing, Institute of Computing Technology,
Chinese Academy of Sciences, Beijing 100190, China
{shizz,mag,yangx}@ics.ict.ac.cn, yuejp@163.com
[2] University of Chinese Academy of Sciences, Beijing 100049, China

Abstract. ABGP is an agent cognitive model, which combines external perception and internal mental state of agents together. The model consists of 4-tuple <Awareness, Belief, Goal, Plan>. For environment awareness a framework named Coding and Combining Features (CCF) is proposed in this paper. The CCF framework combines feature descriptors together based on the compact coding. In the CCF framework firstly compact codes are learned to be robust to complex image content variations. Secondly, the compact codes from multiple information sources are combined by multi-kernel learning to generate the final feature. The experiment results show us that CCF method achieves a better performance in the identification task.

Keywords: Compact coding · Awareness · Agent model ABGP

1 Introduction

Cyborg intelligence is dedicated to integrating artificial intelligence with biological intelligence by tightly connecting machines and biological beings [1]. The key issue is how to collaborate between machines and biological beings? In our project entitled Cognitive Computational Model for Brain Machine integration we use multi-agent collaboration to simulate their behaviors.

We consider that under practical environment the agent should be rational. Rational agents have an explicit representation for their environment and objectives they are trying to achieve. Rationality means that the agent will always perform the most promising actions to achieve its objectives. For a rational agent faced with a complex natural scene, how to get knowledge from scenes to drive their actions? Most agent designer maybe have a common view that either create a virtual scene or set some single inflexible rules for agent to recognize surrounding.

As an internal mental model of agent, BDI model has been well recognized in philosophical and artificial intelligence area. Bratman's philosophical theory was formalized by Cohen and Levesque [2]. In their formalism, intentions are defined in terms of temporal sequences of agent's beliefs and goals. Rao and Georgeff have proposed a possible-worlds formalism for BDI architecture [3]. The abstract architecture they proposed comprises three dynamic data structures representing the agent's beliefs, desires, and intentions, together with an input queue of events. The update operations

© IFIP International Federation for Information Processing 2015
T. Dillon (Ed.): IFIP AI 2015, IFIP AICT 465, pp. 98–107, 2015.
DOI: 10.1007/978-3-319-25261-2_9

on beliefs, desires, and intentions are subject to respective compatibility requirements. These functions are critical in enforcing the formalized constraints upon the agent's mental attitudes. The events the system can recognize include both external events and internal events.

A cognitive model for multi-agent collaboration should consider external perception and internal mental state of agents. Awareness is knowledge created through interaction between an agent and its environment. Endsley pointed out awareness has four basic characteristics [4]:

a) Awareness is knowledge about the state of a particular environment.
b) Environments change over time, so awareness must be kept up to date.
c) People maintain their awareness by interacting with the environment.
d) Awareness is usually a secondary goal—that is, the overall goal is not simply

For internal mental state of agents we can consult BDI model which was conceived by Bratman as a theory of human practical reasoning. Its success is based on its simplicity reducing the explanation framework for complex human behavior to the motivational stance [5]. This means that the causes for actions are always related to human desires ignoring other facets of human cognition such as emotions. Another strength of the BDI model is the consistent usage of folk psychological notions that closely correspond to the way people talk about human behavior.

In terms of above considerations we propose a cognitive model ABGP for multi-agent collaboration through 4-tuple <Awareness, Belief, Goal, Plan>[6]. Awareness is an information pathway connecting to the world (including natural scenes and other agents in multi-agent system). Beliefs can be viewed as the agent's knowledge about its setting and itself. Goals make up the agent's wishes and drive the course of its actions. Plans represent agent's means to achieve its goals. If we expect the agent constructed by ABGP model has an ability to sense directly the natural scenes, a new awareness pathway must to be proposed.

In computer vision, visual feature extraction is vital for object identification, image retrieval, scene classification, etc. These features are complement and should be synthesized together in computer vision applications. For example, edge and texture features are suitable for landscape and building scene classification; shape features are suitable to recognize objects such as apples. However, existing applications mainly focus on one kind of features such as the wildly used SIFT [7] texture feature. To improve the feature discriminabilty, we put forward that complement features corresponding to different reacting regions of brain should be binding together to simulate the brain.

Wu [8] proposed a method to bundle two complement feature detecting methods together, i.e. SIFT [7] and MSER [9]. Xie [10] also bundles two detectors together. However, these two methods are detector binding methods, not considering the description aspects. The description of visual features is vital for the analysis of visual contents. Many of such methods have been proposed to code features into more compact representations, such as binary codes.

For environment awareness we propose a framework named CCF (Coding and Combining Features) to combine feature descriptors together based on the compact coding. In the CCF framework we take advantage of complement feature extracting methods, compact coding methods and multi-kernel hashing together. We encode features into compact binary codes by an effective Locality Preserving Coding method and combine the codes together by multi-kernel hashing. The combined feature achieves a good trade-off between discriminability, robust and learning efficiency. And thus our method achieves a better performance in the experiments.

In previous work we have described agent model ABGP[6]. In this paper we describe especially on environment awareness. This paper is organized as follows. Briefly introduction of agent model ABGP is given in Section 2. Section 3 describes the coding and combining features framework. The experimental results are put into Section 4. Section 5 concludes with a discussion on environment awareness of rational agents.

2   Agent Model ABGP

In computer science and artificial intelligence, agent can be viewed as perceiving its environment information through sensors and acting environment through effectors [11]. A cognitive model for rational agent should especially consider external perception and internal mental state. The external perception as a knowledge is created through interaction between an agent and its world. A cognitive model ABGP (shown as in Figure 1) is represented as a 4-tuple framework as $\langle$Awareness; Belief; Goal; Plan$\rangle$, where awareness is an information pathway connecting to the world and a relationship between agents. Awareness is defined as 2-tuple MA = $\langle$Element, Relation$\rangle$[6].

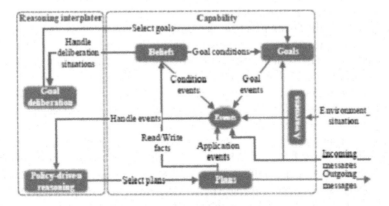

Fig. 1. Agent model ABGP

Belief can be viewed as the agent's knowledge about its environment and itself. Goal represents the concrete motivations that influence an agent's behaviors. Plan is used to achieve agent's goals. Policy can be seen as a state transition function, and multi-agent system changes their state based on policies.

In this paper, we only discuss how to identify who is participating. In order to identify an object we propose a coding and combining features framework described in next section.

3   Coding and Combining Features Framework

3.1   Introduction of the Framework

The CCF Framework process an image into a set of codes, and then bundles the codes together to accomplish recognition or identification   tasks. The model is composed of three steps:

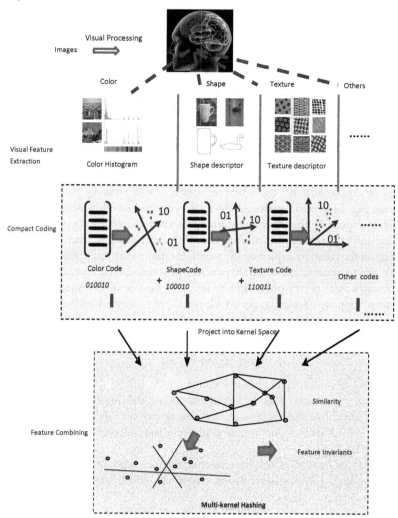

Fig. 2. Coding and Combining Features Framework

1. *Visual Feature Extraction.* Visual features such as color histogram, Gabor filters, intensity histogram, etc. are widely used in content based image analysis. In Figure 2, there are only three different features referred as samples. Actually, most of existing feature e descriptors can be adopted in the model to simulate the visual processing of brain.

2. *Compact Coding*. After various features are extracted, we compact them into efficient and effective codes. To preserve as much information as possible during the coding process, we propose a novel coding method which will be introduced in detail in the next section.
3. *Learning Combined Features*. The codes generated in the compact coding step are then combined by multi-kernel hashing to make a more discriminative feature representation. Since different features such as color, texture impose different information, they are complement and effective in different situations.

3.2   Compact Coding

In this step, our object is not only to encode the features to a more robust and compact codes, but also to bind the features that are visually similar but change slightly in visual contents. We seek a binary coding approach that preserves the visual similarity relationships under the encoding Hamming space. Specifically, we propose a Locality Preserving Coding (LPC) method to learn robust binary codes by exploring the underlying manifold structure of training samples, with effective and efficient optimization.

The objective in this step is to code the visually similar patches into similar binary codes. In this section, we use affine transformation to simulate patches with similar contents but different in scales, slight transitions, and small content variations, as is shown in Figure 3. The other transformations such as lighting, Gaussian noise, scaling, etc can also be used to simulate visually similar patches. Then binary codes are learned on the patch by exploring the manifold structure of patch descriptors.

We aim to preserve the manifold structure of visual similar features when compacting descriptors to binary codes. Let $X=\{x_1,...,x_n\}$ be a set of d-dimensional visual descriptors. Suppose we want to get a k-bit code y_i of x_i, then k hash functions leading to k Hamming embeddings are needed. We use linear projection and threshold to encode X, and then binary code is computed using the following equation:

$$y_i = \text{sign}\,(\,Px_i^T + t\,) \tag{1}$$

where P is a $k*d$ matrix and t is a $k*1$ vector.

The projection matrix P is the key of embedding and threshold t is the key of binarization. To encode the visually similar descriptors into the same binary code, we compute P by solving an optimization problem and utilizing the visual relationships between descriptors.

Given a matrix W with weights characterizing the similarity of two image patches, we want to learn a P to preserve the local structure, which satisfies the following:

$$\text{minimize}: \sum_{ij} \left\| y_i' - y_j' \right\|^2 w_{ij} \tag{2}$$

where y' is the data projected by P, i.e. $y'=Px^T$ and w_{ij} is defined as (3) or (4) :

$$w_{ij} = \begin{cases} \exp(-\left\| x_i - x_j \right\|^2 / \beta), & \text{If } x_i \text{ and } x_j \text{ are visully similar} \\ 0, & \text{Otherwise} \end{cases} \tag{3}$$

$$w_{ij} = \begin{cases} 1, & \text{If } x_i \text{ and } x_j \text{ are visully similar} \\ 0, & \text{Otherwise} \end{cases} \tag{4}$$

The similarity learning method is the spirit of LPP and P can be obtained by solving a generalized Eigen value problem as in [12]. Then we concatenate the generated codes to the final decision code. The similarity between two objects can be measured by the distance between their final decision codes. A smaller distance means the two objects are more similar.

3.3 Learning Combined-Feature

In this section, the codes of different features are combined by multi kernel hashing. Suppose we are given a set of N training binary codes $x^m = [x_1^m, x_2^m ... x_N^m]$ with M different visual features. The hash codes Y with p bits are learned to preserve the manifold structure of visual similar features by multi-kernel hashing. For each feature, let K_{ij} denote the multi-kernel function between the i-th and j-th data, which is linearly combined by kernels for each feature K_{ij}^m. Let $\varphi(\cdot)$ denote the embedding function of the p-th multi-kernel function, the hyperplane vector V_p in the kernel space can be represented as a combination of L landmarks Z_l embedded in corresponding kernel space:

$$V_p = \sum_{l=1}^{L} W_{lp} \varphi(Z_l), l = 1,...L \tag{4}$$

The p-th binary code after multi-kernel hashing is:

$$y_p = sign(V_p^T \varphi(\cdot) + b_p) \tag{5}$$

Then the final combined code after multi-kernel hashing of the compact code $x = [x_1,...x_m]$ is:

$$y = sign(W^T [K(x, Z_1),..., K(x, Z_l)]^T + b)$$

The formulation forces the learned hash functions to preserve the given similarity as much as possible, by optimizing both hyperplane vectors W:

$$\min \frac{1}{2} \sum_{i,j=1}^{N} S_{ij} \|Y_i - Y_j\|_2 + \lambda \|V\|_F^2 \tag{6}$$

$$s.t. \sum_{i=1}^{N} Y_i = 0, \frac{1}{N} \sum_{i=1}^{N} Y_i Y_i^T = 0$$

The optimization problem can be solved by the relaxed problem and details can be found in [13].

The CCF framework can be applied to the object retrieval and recognition task. Take retrieval for example, the similarity between two objects can be measured by the distance of their final decision codes. The hamming distance is used to measure the similarity. A smaller distance means the two objects are more similar in the manifold structure.

4   Experimental Results

In our CCF framework, compact coding and multi-kernel hashing to combine features are two key steps. Firstly, we evaluate the independent compact coding step. Secondly, we evaluate the multi-kernel hashing by combining two different features.

4.1   Compact Coding Evaluation

Dataset. We simulate the affine transformations of images selected from INRIA Holiday, utilize SIFT to detect features and generate visually similar image patches. There are totally 10k groups, some of which are illustrated in Figure 3. Each group of image patches is similar in vision but changes in computer representations. The objective of compact coding is to encode one group of patches into the same binary code. We select 5k groups randomly for training and the rest for testing.

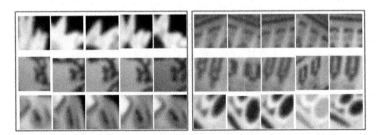

Fig. 3. Samples of evaluation dataset

We compare our compact coding method with LSH (Locality Sensitive Hashing) [14], SH (Spectral Hashing)[15], LDAHash (Linear Discriminant Analysis Hash) [16] which are coding methods widely used in multimedia retrieval task. The experiment conducts image patch retrieval using these methods and our coding method, the results are shown in Figure 4. The LPH refers to our method using equation (3), while LPH-1 refers to the method using equation (4).

Figure 4 uses recall and rate-of-codes-retrieved curve to evaluate the retrieval task. A higher recall means more correct similar patches are found, which indicates the image patch retrieval accuracy. The rate of codes retrieved indicates the noises contained in the final results. And thus a lower rate means lower noises and the number of incorrect patches is smaller. We can conclude from the figure that our compact coding method achieves a better performance in this task. The reason is that our coding method not only utilizes the supervised visual information, but also considers the manifold structure of data.

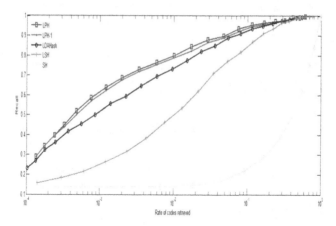

Fig. 4. Comparison of compact coding methods

4.2   Feature Combining Evaluation

Then we evaluate the combined feature on the Ukbench [17] image retrieval dataset, which contains 10,200 images including groups of 4 similar images. In this experiment, we combine texture histogram and color histogram together based on the compact coding. The texture feature is extracted by computing texture histogram from image patches, and the dimensionality is 80. The color feature is extracted by computing quantized color histogram and the dimensionality is 27. And the compact code is of 64-bit, which consumes much less memory.

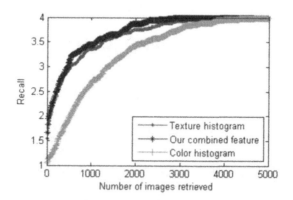

Fig. 5. Combined feature evaluation

From Figure 5, we can see that the combined feature achieves a higher recall than the color histogram and the texture feature. The combined feature utilizes two complementary features and benefit from compact coding, and thus features generated by our CCF framework is more discriminative and robust. Our method is effective with much less memory consumption, which can be used in large-scale applications.

We also use the CIFAR-10 dataset [18] to evaluate multi-kernel hashing based on compact coding, which consists of 60k 32*32 color images in 10 classes with 6k images per class. There are 50k training images and 10k test images. For each image, two features are extracted to evaluate our coding and combining framework, i.e. GIST feature of 384-D and bag of visual words of 300-D quantized from dense SIFT features of 8*8 patches with 4 space overlap. The GIST feature and SIFT features are extracted, compactly coded by LPC and then combined by multi-kernel hashing. The combining method will be evaluated in this experiment.

From the Figure 6 we can see that the precision and recall of our CCF method outperforms LSH with both 16bits and 32bits.

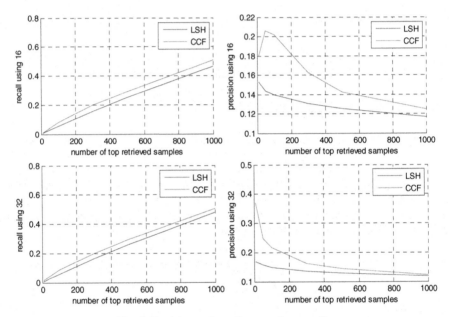

Fig. 6. Precision and recall comparison results

5   Conclusions

We propose a CCF novel feature combining framework to generate a robust and discriminative feature representation with effective coding technique. In the framework, features are encoded into compact codes which represent features with much more information and less units. Then the compact codes are combined to the final discriminative and robust feature by multi-kernel hashing.

The CCF framework is applied to environment awareness for agent model ABGP, which combines external perception and internal mental state. The CCF framework also can be applied many other feature extraction methods. Actually, the weights of different features can be utilized and learned from training samples.

Acknowledgment. This work was supported by the National Program on Key Basic Research Project (973 Program) (No. 2013CB329502), National Natural Science Foundation of China (61035003), National Science and Technology Support Program（2012BA107B02）.

References

1. Wu, Z., Pan, G., Zheng, N.: Cyborg Intelligence. IEEE Intelligent Systems **28**(5), 31–33 (2013)
2. Cohen, P.R., Levesque, H.J.: Intention is choicewith commitment. Artificial Intelligence **42**(2–3), 213–361 (1990)
3. Rao, A.S., Georgeff, M.P.: Modeling rational agents within a BDI-architecture. In: Allen, J., Fikes, R., Sandewall, E. (eds.) Proceedings of the Second International Conference on Principles of Knowledge Representation and Reasoning. Morgan Kaufmann Publishers, San Mateo (1991)
4. Endsley, M.: Toward a Theory of Situation Awareness in Dynamic Systems. Human Factors **37**(1), 32–64 (1995)
5. Pokahr, A., Braubach, L.: The active components approach for distributed systems development. IJPEDS **28**(4), 321–369 (2013)
6. Shi, Z., Zhang, J., Yue, J., Yang, X.: A Cognitive Model for Multi-Agent Collaboration. International Journal of Intelligence Science **4**(1), 1–6 (2014)
7. Lowe, D.: Distinctive image features from scale invariant keypoints. IJCV **60**(2), 91–110 (2004)
8. Wu, Z., Ke, Q., Isard, M., Sun, J.: Bundling Features for Large Scale Partial-Duplicate Web Image Search. In: CVPR 2009 (2009)
9. Matas, J., Chum, O., Urban, M., Pajdla, T.: Robust wide baseline stereo from maximally stable extremal regions. In: BMVC, pp. 384–393 (2002)
10. Xie, H., Gao, K., Zhang, Y., Li, J., Liu, Y., Ren, H.: Effective and efficient image copy detection based on GPU. In: Kutulakos, K.N. (ed.) ECCV 2010 Workshops, Part II. LNCS, vol. 6554, pp. 338–349. Springer, Heidelberg (2012)
11. Shi, Z., Wang, X., Yue, J.: Cognitive Cycle in Mind Model CAM. International Journal of Intelligence Science **1**(2), 25–34 (2011)
12. He, X., Niyogi, P.: Locality preserving projections. In: Neural Information Processing Systems. MIT Press (2003)
13. Liu, X.L., He, J.F., Liu, D., Lang, B.: Compact kernel hashing with multiple features. In: MM 2012 (2012)
14. Datar, M., Immorlica, N., Indyk, P., et al.: Locality-sensitive hashing scheme based on p-stable distributions. In: Proceedings of the 20th annual symposium on Computational geometry (SCG), pp. 253–262 (2004)
15. Weiss, Y., Torralba, A., Fergus, R.: Spectral hashing. In: Proceedings of Neural Information Processing Systems (NIPS), Canada, pp. 1–8 (2008)
16. Strecha, C., Bronstein, A., Bronstein, M., et al.: LDAHash: Improved Matching with Smaller Descriptors. IEEE Trans on PAMI **34**(99), 1–9 (2012)
17. Nister, D., Stewenius, H.: Scalable Recognition with a Vocabulary Tree. Computer Vision and Pattern Recognition (2006)
18. http://www.cs.toronto.edu/~kriz/cifar.html

Evaluation of Recent Computational Approaches in Short-Term Traffic Forecasting

Haofan Yang, Tharam S. Dillon, and Yi-Ping Phoebe Chen[(⊠)]

Department of Computer Science and Information Technology,
La Trobe University, Melbourne, VIC 3086, Australia
Phoebe.Chen@latrobe.edu.au

Abstract. Computational technologies under the domain of intelligent systems are expected to help the rapidly increasing traffic congestion problem in recent traffic management. Traffic management requires efficient and accurate forecasting models to assist real time traffic control systems. Researchers have proposed various computational approaches, especially in short-term traffic flow forecasting, in order to establish reliable traffic patterns models and generate timely prediction results. Forecasting models should have high accuracy and low computational time to be applied in intelligent traffic management. Therefore, this paper aims to evaluate recent computational modeling approaches utilized in short-term traffic flow forecasting. These approaches are evaluated by real-world data collected on the British freeway (M6) from 1st to 30th November in 2014. The results indicate that neural network model outperforms generalized additive model and autoregressive integrated moving average model on the accuracy of freeway traffic forecasting.

Keywords: Computational approach · Short-term traffic forecasting

1   Introduction

Traffic during peak hours in developed and developing countries is usually congested and such problem is apace rising since the past three decades. Computational technologies particularly intelligent systems are expected to help the rapidly increasing traffic congestion problem in recent traffic management. The use of intelligent systems is an important trend in traffic management, and its objective is to provide innovative services to transportation development and enable various users to better use of transport networks. Advances in computing and communications technologies promote using intelligent systems to manage many problems in transportation, especially the traffic congestion [1-3]. Congestion can be reduced by redistributing traffic spatially and temporally. To achieve traffic flow redistribution, it is necessary to get future traffic conditions [4, 5]. The authors in [6] also emphasized that it is necessary to continuously forecast the traffic conditions for short time ahead to enable dynamic traffic control. These cause establishing efficient and accurate traffic flow forecasting models to become an important issue in traffic management.

© IFIP International Federation for Information Processing 2015
T. Dillon (Ed.): IFIP AI 2015, IFIP AICT 465, pp. 108–116, 2015.
DOI: 10.1007/978-3-319-25261-2_10

Lieu, et al. [7, 8] stated that the way to establish a reliable and efficient intelligent traffic system relies on providing continuous information of the traffic conditions over time. Such traffic information need to be updated in a timely fashion and should generate projections on the expected traffic networks [9]. In the new era of intelligent traffic systems, research has focus on establishing forecasting models to manage the traffic networks [10-12]. Many computational approaches have been commonly applied to build forecasting models, such as neural network (NN), generalized additive model (GAM), and autoregressive integrated moving average (ARIMA) [6, 13-16]. In this paper, above approaches are applied to the traffic data collected on the British freeway (M6) from 1st to 30th November in 2014 for evaluation. We evaluate three different approaches and report on their performance. The rest of this paper is organized as follows. Section 2 describes the computational modeling approaches used in this study. Section 3 explains the experimental design. Section 4 discusses the experiment results. Finally, the conclusion is given in Section 5.

2   Description of Used Computational Modeling Approaches

2.1   Neural Network (NN)

NN is a kind of information processing technique, and it can be trained to learn relationships in a dataset. The NN model has been applied in short-term traffic forecasting for many years, and it has been proven to be effective in solving problems that existing complex relationships, such as traffic flow forecasting [13, 17-19]. Since the traffic data with lumpiness may reduce the generalization capability on the short-term traffic flow forecasting on unseen data [20], we applied the exponential smoothing method [21, 22] to remove lumpiness in the collected traffic data. After removing the lumpiness, a three-layer feed-forward NN with levenberg-Marquardt algorithm was trained to establish a short-term traffic forecasting model. The traffic data is collected from n sensing stations $(S_1, S_2, S_3,...,S_n)$, which are located on the freeway (M6). S_i captures two traffic condition measures, i.e., the average vehicle speed $\hat{V}_i(t)$ and the average headway $\hat{h}_i(t)$ between time t and time $t+T_S$, where T_S is the sampling time. Future traffic conditions can be forecasted by the NN model, according to the current and past traffic conditions. The current traffic condition is denoted by the current average speed $\hat{V}_i(t)$ and current average headway $\hat{h}_i(t)$. The past traffic condition is indicated by the past average speed $\hat{V}_i(t - kT_s)$ and past average headway $\hat{h}_i(t - kT_s)$, which was collected by Si at time $(t - kT_s)$ with $i=1,2,3,...,n$ and $k=1,2,3,...,p$, whereas the past traffic data within p sampling time period are collected. The future traffic condition can then be generated by the NN model, which is indicated by $\hat{h}_L(t + mT_s)$ passing through the Lth sensing station S_L at time $(t + mT_s)$, where future traffic condition with m sampling time ahead is forecasted. The NN model is formulated as:

$$\hat{h}_L(t + mT_s) = \sum_{i=1}^{n} \sum_{j=1}^{M} \left[\beta_{j,i}^V \left(\gamma_{0,j,i}^V + \sum_{k=1}^{p} \gamma_{k,j,i}^V V_i(t - kT_s) \right) \right.$$
$$\left. + \beta_{j,i}^h \left(\gamma_{0,j,i}^h + \sum_{k=1}^{p} \gamma_{k,j,i}^h h_i(t - kT_s) \right) \right] + \alpha_0 \qquad (1)$$

where M is the number of nodes in the hidden layer; $()$ is the activation function of the hidden set (sigmoid function is used in this study); $\beta_{j,i}^V$, $\beta_{j,i}^h$, $\gamma_{0,j,i}^V$, $\gamma_{0,j,i}^h$, $\gamma_{k,j,i}^V$, $\gamma_{k,j,i}^h$, and α_0 are the parameters of the *NN* model.

2.2   Generalized Additive Model (*GAM*)

The *GAM* has the ability to allow non-parametric fits with relaxed assumptions between predicted and actual values. With this ability, the *GAM* can provide better fits to data than purely parametric models. The *GAM* is based on the additive model (*AM*), which is a nonparametric regression method that assumes the mean of a response variable depends on predictors by a nonlinear function. The *AM* relates a univariate response variable to a set of other response variables. The *GAM* extends the generalized *AM* which assumes linear dependence, by allowing the dependence of the response variable to be nonlinear [23]. The *GAM* is generalizing the *AM* to allow the response variable to follow an exponential family distribution [24, 25] along with a link function. Given a data set $\{y_i, x_{i1}, x_{i2}, ..., x_{ip}\}_{i=1}^{n}$ of data size n, where y_i and x_i are the ith observations of the traffic flow, the *AM* is formulated as:

$$y_i = \sum_{j=1}^{p} f_j(x_{ij}) + \varepsilon_i \qquad (2)$$

where $f_j(x_{ij})$ is a smooth function of the ith observation of covariate j, and ε_i is the residual. With a link function G, the *GAM* can be structured as:

$$G\left(E(y_i | x_{i1}, x_{i2}, ..., x_{ip}) \right) = f_0 + \sum_{j=1}^{p} f_j(x_{ij}) + \varepsilon_i \qquad (3)$$

where f_0 is the intercept that is equal to the overall mean of the y_i [23, 25]. In this study, a local scoring algorithm which maximizes a likelihood function is used to estimate the used smooth functions in *GAM*. Also, the generalized cross-sectional validation approach is used to avoid over-fitting in the short-term traffic flow forecasting.

2.3   Auto-Regressive Integrated Moving Average (*ARIMA*)

The *ARIMA* model, one of the most popular time series approach applied in traffic flow forecasting, is generally referred as *ARIMA (p, d, q)*, where *p, d,* and *q* are non-negative integers [26]. *p, d,* and *q* refer to the order of the autoregressive, integrated, and moving average parts of the model, respectively. To empirically create a proper model, we followed the Box-Jenkins *ARIMA* modeling procedure which consists of the following steps: identification, estimation, diagnostic checking, and forecasting [27]. Through continuous modification, the most proper forecasting model can be generated.

In the identification step, the collected traffic data is assessed to determine whether it is stationary. Autocorrelation function (*ACF*) and Partial Autocorrelation Function (*PACF*) are used to detect it [28]. If the collected traffic data is not stationary, the differencing approach is applied. The value *d* is the lowest order of differencing applied to achieve stationary. The second step is to decide whether *AR(p)* or *MA(q)* should be used in the model. According to the *ACF* and *PACF* plots of the differenced series, it is possible to tentatively identify the value *p* and/or *q*. The error residuals can be calculated when the candidate model *ARIMA (p, d, q)* is estimated. The candidate model is further tested by Akaike Information Criterion (*AIC*) and Schwartz's Bayesian Criterion (*SBC*) in diagnostic checking step [29]. The lower value of *AIC* and *SBC*, the more suitable *ARIMA (p, d, q)* should be. Q-test is also used to determine whether the estimated model is suitable. If the candidate model cannot pass the test, the process should go back to the identification step to develop a better model. The candidate model which passed diagnostic checking is set as the used *ARIMA* model in short-term traffic flow forecasting. In the *ARIMA* model, we predict $\hat{h}_L(t + mT_s)$, the average traffic flow at the Lth sensing station S_L at time $(t + mT_s)$, where future traffic condition with *m* sampling time ahead is forecasted based on the past traffic flow condition. The past traffic flow condition P_{tf} is defined as

$$P_{tf} = (1 - L)^d \hat{h}_L(t + mT_s) \tag{4}$$

L is the lag operation and the *ARIMA* model is structured as:

$$(1 - \sum_{i=1}^{p} \Phi_i L_i) P_{tf} = (1 + \sum_{i=1}^{q} \theta_i L_i) \varepsilon_T \tag{5}$$

where *p* is the order of autoregressive and *q* is the order of moving average. Φ_k and θ_k are the parameters of the autoregressive and moving average parts, respectively. ε_T are error terms for the stationary distribution.

3   Experimental Design

The traffic flow data was collected from the British traffic warehouse, and it was captured by ANPR cameras, in-vehicle GPS and inductive loops built into the road surface located between junctions, J40 and J41, of the freeway M6 in the United Kingdom from 1st to 30th November in 2014. The main aim of traffic flow forecasting is to help for reducing traffic congestion, therefore the peak traffic period on the business days should be the main target. The traffic time periods are set to 15-minute intervals in the day which also refers to 0 to 95 where 0 indicates 00:00 to 00:15 and 95 refers to 23:45 to 24:00. The collected traffic data was analyzed and it was found all business days had similar traffic headway distribution as shown in Fig. 1. The figure illustrates how the data have daily seasonal patterns, which are periodically repeated. The peak traffic flow condition was occurred in mornings between 7:00 and 9:30 (time period 28 to 37) and evenings between 17:00 and 19:30 (time period 68 to 77) on the business days.

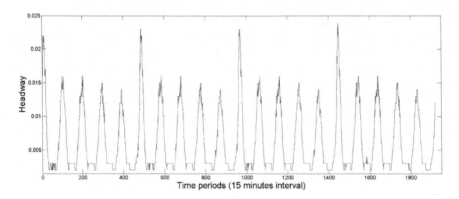

Fig. 1. Traffic headway distribution on the business day between 1st to 30th November in 2014. The time period index (0 to 1920) starts on Monday 00:15 at 3rd November and ends on Friday 24:00 at 28th November in 2014 with 96 intervals (15-minutes intervals) per day.

To train the models (*NN*, *GAM*, and *ARIMA*) of the selected road section, we excluded weekend traffic data since it has different daily patterns. The total number of days used for evaluation is 20 (business days between 3rd to 28th November). The significance level is set to 5% and the confidence interval is 95% in all analyses used in this study. The remained traffic data was divided into two subsets. The data of first subset, namely the training set, was used for establishing the *NN*, *GAM*, and *ARIMA* models. The data of second subset, namely the test set, was applied to evaluate the generalization capability of the trained models. The business days of the first three weeks in November 2014 were set in the training set and the business days of the last week in November 2014 were concluded in the test set. For the time period with 15-minute intervals, training data set and testing data set contain 1440 (3*5*96) data and 480 (1*5*96) data, respectively. Since the generalization capability on traffic flow forecasting would be improved by removing the lumpiness from the raw traffic data, we applied the exponential smoothing method to remove lumpiness in the collected data before applying the data to develop proposed models.

In order to evaluate the accuracy and efficiency of the *NN*, *GAM*, and *ARIMA* models, the performance of these models was evaluated by Mean Absolute Percentage Error (MAPE) and Root Mean Square Error (RMSE). MAPE and RMSE indicate the mean and the sample standard deviation of the differences between observed values and predicted values, respectively.

4   Experiment Results and Discussion

Since the main target in this study is the peak traffic period on the business days, we evaluate the forecast an hour ahead (in the peak traffic period 34 to 37 or 74 to 77) using the models developed in the training phase. The traffic flow conditions on the road section M6-J40 to M6-J41 from the previous one and half hours (in the peak traffic period 28 to 33 or 68 to 73) of the same peak traffic period (morning or evening peak) are used, i.e., the previous 6 records of a peak traffic period are used to predict 4 records ahead during the same peak traffic period. The forecasting models (*NN*, *GAM*, and *ARIMA*) are evaluated in different business days using the testing data set. The forecasted results are compared with real observations in order to know the performance of each model which is evaluated by the MAPE and RMSE. The *ARIMA* model considers the number of lags to forecast a future value, therefore it is used to forecast the time $(t + 2 * mT_s)$ value.

Table 1. Comparison of forecasting models based on MAPE in peak traffic periods. Morning peak 34 to 37 indicates 08:30 to 09:30 and evening peak 74 to 77 denotes 18:30 to 19:30.

Traffic	Model	MAPE%				
Peak period		Mon	Tue	Wed	Thu	Fri
Morning peak 34 to 37	*NN*	2.19	1.85	1.99	2.11	2.61
	GAM	2.76	4.02	4.28	3.36	3.63
	ARIMA	13.32	15.17	16.05	14.54	14.91
Evening peak 74 to 77	*NN*	1.73	2.08	2.24	2.83	1.90
	GAM	3.04	3.88	3.61	2.98	4.11
	ARIMA	17.43	17.58	15.68	16.38	17.09

The forecasting performance of *NN*, *GAM*, and *ARIMA* models applied to peak traffic periods of the testing data set are presented in Table 1 and Table 2. For the comparison results displayed in Table 1 and Table 2, we notice that the MAPEs and RMSEs of the *NN* model are smaller than those of the GAM and ARIMA models during the morning peak and evening peak. Fig.2. shows the comparison between the observed traffic headway values and the predicted headway values which are generated by *NN*, *GAM* or *ARIMA* models on Monday 24th November 2014. The comparison between the observed traffic headway values and the predicted headway values on 25th, 26th, 27th, and 28th November (Tuesday to Friday) presents similar results as Monday 24th.

Table 2. Comparison of forecasting models based on RMSE in peak traffic periods. Morning peak 34 to 37 indicates 08:30 to 09:30 and evening peak 74 to 77 denotes 18:30 to 19:30.

Traffic	Model	RMSE				
Peak period		Mon	Tue	Wed	Thu	Fri
Morning peak 34 to 37	NN	1.20	1.01	1.36	1.05	1.14
	GAM	2.38	1.54	3.05	1.56	1.68
	ARIMA	5.60	6.18	4.92	7.60	6.57
Evening peak 74 to 77	NN	1.15	1.20	1.72	1.41	1.53
	GAM	2.65	1.69	2.85	1.88	2.03
	ARIMA	7.43	7.26	4.91	8.66	7.59

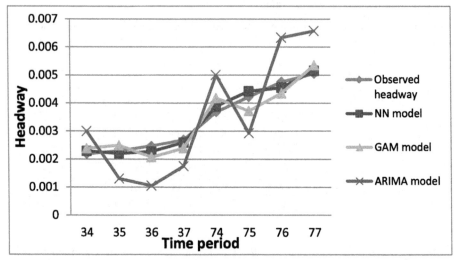

Fig. 2. Headway comparison between observed and predicted values on Monday 24th November 2014. 34 to 37 and 74 to 77 refer to 08:30 to 09:30 and 18:30 to 19:30, respectively.

Both Tables and Fig. 2 show that the *NN* model performs much better than the other models as its predicted headway values are close to the observed headway values. Moreover, its MAPE and RMSE values are less than *GAM* and *ARIMA* models.

5   Conclusion

Due to the fact that traffic congestion problem is rapidly increasing, it is urgent to establish intelligent traffic control systems that can redistribute the traffic flow spatially and temporally. In order to reach it, an efficient and accurate forecasting model is necessary to assist real time traffic control systems. Research has applied many computational approaches on short-term traffic forecasting to build forecasting models. While the traffic flow data of a road link can be collected much easier than before, selecting appropriate computational approaches to deal with the demand of forecasting accuracy and efficiency is getting significant. In this paper, we proposed to evaluate some computational approaches in short-term traffic flow forecasting. From the experiment results, we found that on forecasting accuracy, *NN* model outperforms *GAM* and *ARIMA* models on forecasting accuracy of the short-term freeway traffic forecasting.

References

1. Gu, H., Wang, W., Hu, Y., Qiao, L., Zhan, F.: Study on the intelligent transport system and social economic development. In: CICTP: Multimodal Transportation Systems—Convenient, Safe, Cost-Effective, Efficient, 2012, pp. 845–855 (2012)
2. Ben-Akiva, M.E., Gao, S., Wei, Z., Wen, Y.: A dynamic traffic assignment model for highly congested urban networks. Transportation Research Part C: Emerging Technologies **24**, 62–82 (2012)
3. Hamilton, A., Waterson, B., Cherrett, T., Robinson, A., Snell, I.: The evolution of urban traffic control: changing policy and technology. Transportation planning and technology **36**, 24–43 (2013)
4. Daganzo, C.F.: A behavioral theory of multi-lane traffic flow. Part II: Merges and the onset of congestion. Transportation Research Part B: Methodological **36**, 159–169 (2002)
5. Kamal, S., Imura, J.-I., Hayakawa, T., Ohata, A., Aihara, K.: Smart Driving of a Vehicle Using Model Predictive Control for Improving Traffic Flow. IEEE Transactions on Intelligent Transportation Systems **15**, 878–888 (2014)
6. Daraghmi, Y.A., Chih-Wei, Y., Tsun-Chieh, C.: Negative Binomial Additive Models for Short-Term Traffic Flow Forecasting in Urban Areas. IEEE Transactions on Intelligent Transportation Systems **15**, 784–793 (2014)
7. Lieu, H., Gartner, N., Messer, C., Rathi, A.: Traffic flow theory. Public Roads **62**, 45–47 (1999)
8. Lieu, H.C.: Traffic estimation and prediction system. 0738-6826 (2000)
9. Vlahogianni, E.I., Golias, J.C., Karlaftis, M.G.: Short-term traffic forecasting: Overview of objectives and methods. Transport reviews **24**, 533–557 (2004)
10. Zhang, Y., Zhang, Y., Haghani, A.: A hybrid short-term traffic flow forecasting method based on spectral analysis and statistical volatility model. Transportation Research Part C: Emerging Technologies **43**, 65–78 (2014)
11. Wu, S., Yang, Z., Zhu, X., Yu, B.: Improved k-nn for Short-Term Traffic Forecasting Using Temporal and Spatial Information. Journal of Transportation Engineering **140** (2014)
12. Zhang, X., Onieva, E., Perallos, A., Osaba, E., Lee, V.C.: Hierarchical fuzzy rule-based system optimized with genetic algorithms for short term traffic congestion prediction. Transportation Research Part C: Emerging Technologies **43**, 127–142 (2014)
13. Chan, K.Y., Dillon, T., Chang, E., Singh, J.: Prediction of short-term traffic variables using intelligent swarm-based neural networks. IEEE Transactions on Control Systems Technology **21**, 263–274 (2013)
14. Chen, C., Hu, J., Meng, Q., Zhang, Y.: Short-time traffic flow prediction with ARIMA-GARCH model. In: Intelligent Vehicles Symposium (IV), pp. 607–612. IEEE (2011)
15. Tjondronegoro, D.W., Chen, Y.-P.: Knowledge-discounted event detection in sports video. IEEE Transactions on Systems, Man and Cybernetics, Part A: Systems and Humans **40**, 1009–1024 (2010)

16. Nahar, J., Chen, Y.-P.P., Ali, S.: Kernel-based naive bayes classifier for breast cancer prediction. Journal of biological systems **15**, 17–25 (2007)
17. Chan, K.Y., Khadem, S., Dillon, T.S., Palade, V., Singh, J., Chang, E.: Selection of significant on-road sensor data for short-term traffic flow forecasting using the Taguchi method. IEEE Transactions on Industrial Informatics **8**, 255–266 (2012)
18. Vlahogianni, E.I., Karlaftis, M.G.: Testing and comparing neural network and statistical approaches for predicting transportation time series. Transportation Research Record: Journal of the Transportation Research Board **2399**, 9–22 (2013)
19. Vanajakshi, L., Rilett, L.R.: A comparison of the performance of artificial neural networks and support vector machines for the prediction of traffic speed. In: Intelligent Vehicles Symposium, pp. 194–199. IEEE (2004)
20. Chan, K.Y., Dillon, T.S., Singh, J., Chang, E.: Neural-network-based models for short-term traffic flow forecasting using a hybrid exponential smoothing and Levenberg–Marquardt algorithm. IEEE Transactions on Intelligent Transportation Systems **13**, 644–654 (2012)
21. DeLurgio, S.A.: Forecasting principles and applications (1998)
22. Wanas, N., Auda, G., Kamel, M.S., Karray, F.: On the optimal number of hidden nodes in a neural network. In: IEEE Canadian Conference on Electrical and Computer Engineering, 1998, pp. 918–921 (1998)
23. Hastie, T.J., Tibshirani, R.J.: Generalized additive models, vol. 43. CRC Press (1990)
24. Wood, S.: Generalized additive models: an introduction with R. CRC press (2006)
25. Wood, S.N., Goude, Y., Shaw, S.: Generalized additive models for large data sets. Journal of the Royal Statistical Society: Series C (Applied Statistics) **64**, 139–155 (2015)
26. Williams, B.M., Hoel, L.A.: Modeling and forecasting vehicular traffic flow as a seasonal ARIMA process: Theoretical basis and empirical results. Journal of transportation engineering **129**, 664–672 (2003)
27. Pankratz, A.: Forecasting with univariate Box-Jenkins models: Concepts and cases, vol. 224. John Wiley & Sons (2009)
28. Liu, L.-M.: Identification of seasonal ARIMA models using a filtering method. Communications in Statistics-Theory and Methods **18**, 2279–2288 (1989)
29. Claeskens, G., Hjort, N.L.: Model selection and model averaging, vol. 330. Cambridge University Press, Cambridge (2008)

Intelligent Decision Support Systems

A Framework for Interestingness Measures for Association Rules with Discrete and Continuous Attributes Based on Statistical Validity

Izwan Nizal Mohd Shaharanee[✉] and Jastini Mohd Jamil

School of Quantitative Sciences, Universiti Utara Malaysia, UUM, 06010 Sintok, Malaysia
{nizal,jastini}@uum.edu.my

Abstract. Assessing rules with interestingness measures is the pillar of successful application of association rules discovery. However, association rules discovered are large in number, some of which are not considered as interesting or significant for the application at hand. In this paper, we present a systematic approach to ascertain the discovered rules, and provide a precise statistical approach supporting this framework. Furthermore, considering that many interestingness measures exist, we propose and compare two established approaches in selecting relevant attributes for the rules prior to rule generation. The proposed strategy combines data mining and statistical measurement techniques, including redundancy analysis, sampling and multivariate statistical analysis, to discard the non-significant rules. In addition to that, we consider real world datasets which are characterized by the uniform and non-uniform data/items distribution with mixture of measurement level throughout the data/items. The proposed unified framework is applied on these datasets to demonstrate its effectiveness in discarding many of the redundant or non-significant rules, while still preserving the high accuracy of the rule set as a whole.

Keywords: Data mining · Interesting rules · Statistical analysis

1 Introduction

Data mining or knowledge discovery from data (KDD) is known for its capabilities in offering systematic ways in acquiring useful rules and patterns from large quantities of data. The rules derived from data mining application are considered interesting and useful if they are comprehensible, valid on tests and new data with some degree of certainty, potentially useful, actionable, and novel [1]. [2] claims that the majority of data mining/machine learning type patterns are rule based in nature with a well defined structure, such as rules derived from decision trees and association rules. The most common patterns that can be evaluated by interestingness measures include association rules, classification rules, and summaries [3]. Association rule mining is one of the most popular data mining techniques widely used for discovering interesting associations and correlations between data elements in a diverse range of applications [4]. The association rule mining techniques are different from each other, but a commonality that remains is that all the frequent patterns are first extracted and then

© IFIP International Federation for Information Processing 2015
T. Dillon (Ed.): IFIP AI 2015, IFIP AICT 465, pp. 119–128, 2015.
DOI: 10.1007/978-3-319-25261-2_11

association rules are formed from such patterns. Frequent pattern extraction plays an important part in generating good and interesting rules, and is considered the most difficult and complex task. Different methods have been proposed for discovering interesting rules from data and have been categorized into three main classes, namely objective, subjective and semantic measures [1-3].

Our work in the area of rules interestingness measures is motivated by the objective interestingness measures which are based on probability theory, statistics and information theory. Various objective interestingness criteria have been used to limit the nature of rules extracted, as explained in [3, 6]. Works such as [7, 8] have proposed and successfully developed two approaches, namely multiple support and relative support for generating rules for significant rare data that appears infrequent in the database but is highly associated with specific data. Mutual Information and J-Measures are common information theory approaches in objective interestingness measure [9]. A number of researchers have anticipated an assessment on pattern discovery by applying a statistical significance test as discussed in [6].

Assessing whether a rule satisfies a particular constraint is accompanied by a risk that the rule will satisfy the constraint with respect to the sample data but not with respect to the whole data distribution [10]. As such, the rules may not reflect the "real" association between the underlying attributes. The hypotheses reflected in the generated rules must be validated by a statistical methodology for them to be useful in practice, because the nature of data mining techniques is data driven [11]. However, even if the rules satisfy appropriate statistical tests, it can still be the case that the underlying association is caused purely by a statistical coincidence [12].

The contributions of the work presented in this paper, is in developing systematic ways to verify the usefulness of rules obtained from association rules mining using statistical analysis. A unified framework is proposed, that combines several techniques to access the quality of rules, and remove any redundant and unnecessary rules. Initial ideas and preliminary results were presented earlier in [6, 13]. Several extensions and refinements took place in regards to the method being applicable to more realistic datasets including complex data types, infrequent items and uneven attribute value distribution. Furthermore, a comparison of the statistical measure used in our framework with the popular Mutual Information measure is included. The rest of the paper is organized as follows. Section 2, briefly overviews some related works and defines the problem of ascertaining the discovered rules. In Section 3, we describe our proposed framework. The framework is evaluated using real world datasets and some experimental findings and explanation are given in Section 4. Section 5 concludes the paper and describes our ongoing works in this field of study.

2   Related Works

Association rule mining in its most fundamental structure is to discover interesting relationships among items in a given dataset under minimum support and confidence conditions. Commonly used example is in market basket analysis, where an association rule $X \Rightarrow Y$ means if a consumer buys the set of items X, then he/she probably also buys items Y. These items are typically referred to as itemsets [14]. The problem of finding association rules $X \Rightarrow Y$ was first introduced in [5, 15] as a data mining task of finding frequently co-occurring items in a large Boolean transaction database. Let $I = \{i_1, i_2, ..., i_m\}$ be a set of items. Each transaction T is a set of items, such that $T \subseteq I$. An association rule is a condition of the form of $X \Rightarrow Y$ where $X \subseteq I$ and $Y \subseteq I$ are two sets of items. The support of a rule $X \Rightarrow Y$ is the number of transactions that contain both X and Y, while the confidence of a rule $X \Rightarrow Y$ is the number of transactions containing X, that also contain Y.

In this research we employed an efficient breadth-first method in generating candidate set called Apriori algorithm [16]. The generation of all possible rules was essential in ascertaining the quality of the rules. As this established approach is based on the user specifying the constraints such as support and confidence that must be satisfied. Still, [7, 8] argue that for a real large database that is often comprised of either relatively frequent/infrequent items, using multiple and relative support should be considered.

The rules satisfying the standard support and confidence constraints are often too numerous to be utilized efficiently and effectively for the application at hand [17]. Many patterns from the frequent pattern set are often redundant. Thus we discussed in detailed two useful approaches in handling this redundant problem in [6]. In the datasets where there is a predefined class label (i.e. classification tasks), frequent pattern mining can contribute to discovering strong associations between occurring attribute and class values. In [18] the potential usage of frequent pattern mining for classification problem was investigated and successfully applied to the problem. Their approach discovered classification rules by directly discovering the frequent patterns from the datasets with predefined class labels. The results reported were promising since the discovered knowledge model had high accuracy and efficiency for the classification problem.

3   Proposed Method

Although there are various criteria in determining the usefulness of rules [1, 2, 17] the measures usually just reflect the usefulness of rules with respect to the specific database being observed [10]. The data mining approaches consider the whole search space to find all possible pattern/rules satisfying specific criteria (i.e. association rules). While these criteria, offer some constrains in discovering strong patterns/rules, many misleading, uninteresting and insignificant rules in that domains may still be produced [1]. This problem arises because some association rules are discovered due to pure coincidence resulting from certain randomness in the particular dataset being analyzed. Statistics has previously addressed the issues of how to separate out the random effects to determine if the measured association (or difference in other areas) is significant [22, 23]. Thus additional measures based on statistical independence and correlation analysis are needed to ensure that the results have a sound statistical basis and are not purely random coincidence. The statistical approach offers a firm way of identifying significant rules that are statistically valid. Therefore, the motivation behind our proposed method is to investigate how data mining and statistical measurement techniques can be combined to arrive at more reliable and interesting set of rules. Generally speaking we interpret interesting rules as those rules that have a sound statistical basis and are not redundant. Such an approach requires sampling process, hypothesis development, model building and finally a measurement using statistical analysis techniques to verify and ascertain the usefulness and quality of the rules discovered. This will filter out the redundant, misleading, random and coincidentally occurring rules, while at the same time the accuracy of the rule set will still be sustained.

3.1   Conceptual Framework

Figure 1 shows the proposed framework. The dataset is first divided into two partitions. The first partition is used for association rule generation and statistical evaluation, while the second partition acts as a sample data drawn from the database, used to verify the accuracy of discovered rules. To ensure clean and consistent data, standard preprocessing techniques are applied. These preprocessing techniques include the removal of missing values and discretization of attributes with continuous values. As the next step, we determine the relevance of attributes by classifying their importance to characterize an association. A powerful technique for this purpose is the Symmetrical Tau [19], which is a statistical-heuristic feature selection criterion. It measures the capability of an attribute in predicting the class of another attribute. The measure is based on the probabilities of one attribute value occurring together with the value of the second attribute. [19] define the Symmetrical Tau measure for the capability of input attribute in predicting the class attribute. Higher values of the Tau measure would indicate better discriminating criterions (features) for the class that is to be predicted in the domain. Symmetrical Tau has many more desirable properties in comparison to other feature selection techniques, as was reported in [19].

In Section 4.2 we evaluate the capabilities of Symmetrical Tau as the determinant of relevance attributes by comparing it with an information-theoretic measure. The information-theoretic measures are principally comprehensible and useful since they can be interpreted in terms of information. For a rule interestingness measure, the relation is interesting when the antecedent provides a great deal of information about the consequent [20]. Although several information-theoretic measures exist, we only compared Symmetrical Tau with Mutual Information measurement technique. The Mutual Information is based on information theory to evaluate rules. This approach describes how much information one random variable tells about another one [21]. The definition of Mutual Information is based on [9]. The features selection technique is utilized in our approach to provide the relative usefulness of attributes in predicting the value of the class attribute, and discard any of the attributes whose relevance value is low. This would prevent the generation of rules which then would need to be discarded anyway once it was found that they comprise of some irrelevant attributes.

The rules are then generated based on the minimum support and confidence framework. However, the application of minimum support assumes that all items in the data are of the same nature and/have similar frequency in the database. This will encounter problems given that the frequency distribution of the attribute values or items in the dataset can be significantly different [7]. [8] assert that the data distribution in database may somehow occur either relatively frequently or not, uniformly or non-uniformly distributed according to the characteristics of the database. In response to this rare items problem, several researchers proposed and successfully developed a solution such as multiple minimum support [7] and relative support [8]. For comparison purpose, we apply both relative support and classical Apriori algorithm framework for association rules mining generation. This is to ensure that we treat the dataset that contains rare items correctly, and this will be demonstrated in the experiments provided in Section 4.3.

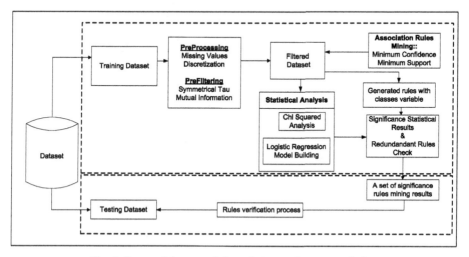

Fig. 1. Proposed framework for rule interestingness analysis.

The discovered rules are then ascertained with statistical techniques. For associations between categorical and continuous variables there are several inferential methods involved. Chi-squared analysis is often used to measure the correlation between items. For a given chi-squared values it can be used to determine if the correlation is statistically significant [1]. The logistic regression methods have become an integral component of any data analysis concerned with describing the relationship between a target variable and one or more input variables [22]. Logistics regression is used to estimate the probability that a particular outcome will occur. The coefficients are estimated using a statistical technique called maximum likelihood estimation. These coefficient values are useful in testing the statistical significance of input variables towards target variables [23]. The interpretation of regression coefficient in terms of odd ratios is a familiar concept in analysis of categorical data [23]. The selection of logistic regression model involves two competing goals: the model should be complex enough to fit the data well, while at the same time simpler models are preferred since they are easier to interpret and are expected to have better generalization [22].

We also use some constraint measurement techniques in order to discard the existence of redundant rules [6]. The combination of these rule ascertaining strategies will facilitate the association rule mining framework to determine the right and high quality rules.

4   Experimental Results

The evaluation of the unification framework is performed using the Adult, Iris and Wine dataset, which are real world datasets obtained form UCI Machine Learning Repository. Since all the datasets used are supervised which reflects a classification problem, we have chosen the target variable as the right hand side/consequence of the association rules discovered during association rule mining analysis. In this section, we first show how we handle continuous and discrete attributes. Then we compare two established features selection algorithms namely Symmetrical Tau and Mutual Information in term of their feature subset selection capabilities. Next, we discuss the effect of the frequent and infrequent item in dataset towards the framework. Finally we demonstrate the whole performance of the framework towards both datasets.

4.1   Discrete and Continuous Attributes

For many real-world problems, the forms of the input and target attributes emerge form wide range of measurement levels. In handling these types of attributes, we apply the binning approach in improving the boundary of the continuous variables. These bound are created to reflect the upper and lower values for the input variables [24]. For all continuous attributes in Adult, Iris and Wine, we apply equal depth binning approach methods. This equal depth binning approach will ensure that, we have a manageable data sizes by reducing the number of distinct values per attributes [1]. Other discrete attributes in Adult dataset were preserved in original state.

4.2   Comparing Symmetrical Tau (ST) with Mutual Information (MI)

ST and MI are capable of defining irrelevant attributes; they are different from each other in terms of their approach as aforementioned in Section 3.1. Throughout the

Table 1. Comparison between ST and MI for Adult Dataset (Initial Proportion)

# of Values	Variables	ST Values	# of Values	Variable	MI Values
7	Marital Status	0.1448	6	Relationships	0.1662
6	Relationship	0.1206	7	Marital Status	0.1575
6	Capital Gain	0.0706	16	Education	0.0934
8	Education Number	0.0688	14	Occupation	0.0932
16	Education	0.0528	8	Education Number	0.0900
2	Sex	0.0470	10	Age	0.0894
14	Occupation	0.0469	10	Hours Per Week	0.0545
10	Age	0.0432	6	Capital Gain	0.0475
5	Capital Loss	0.0361	2	Sex	0.0374
10	Hours Per Week	0.0354	5	Capital Loss	0.0238
7	Work Class	0.0166	7	Work Class	0.0171
5	Race	0.0085	41	Native Country	0.0093
41	Native Country	0.0077	5	Race	0.0083
10	FNLWGT	0.0002	10	FNLWGT	0.0002

experiment as shown in Table 1, we found that MI approach favors variables with more values. This observation is in accord with [20]. On the contrary, the procedure based on ST produces a more stable variables selection which is not in favor to any specific variables criterion. This is in agreement with the claim in [19, 25, 26], of ST being fair towards handling of multi-valued variables.

4.3   Unified Target Data and Rare Target Data Problems

As mention in Section 3.1, [8] assert that the data distribution in database may some-how occur either relatively frequently or not according to the database's characteris-tics. In response to this, we compared the dataset that contains both unified target data and rare target data.

Table 2. Rules accuracy for Adult data

Experimental Approaches	Dataset Description	Rule #	Type of Statistical Analysis	Accuracy	
				Training	Testing
Initial Proportion	Training : 30162 records	164	Initial rules	86.75%	86.87%
	Testing : 15060 records	53	Statistical Analysis	87.73%	87.92%
		42	Redundancy Check	87.99%	88.13%
Balanced Data	Training : 30162~15016 records	421	Initial rules	71.55%	60.56%
		51	Statistical Analysis	73.87%	58.28%
	Testing : 15060 records	30	Redundancy Check	74.00%	63.80%
Replication Data	Training : 30162~45178 records	255	Initial rules	71.65%	59.86%
		51	Statistical Analysis	73.64%	58.28%
	Testing : 15060 records	32	Redundancy Check	73.61%	61.70%
*Multiple Support	Training: 30162 records	164	Initial rules	86.75%	86.87%
	Testing : 15060 records	53	Statistical Analysis	87.73%	87.92%
		42	Redundancy Check	87.99%	88.13%
	*5% as 2nd support	42+*4	Redundancy Check	87.34%	87.47%

Table 2 shows four experiments done for Adult dataset. For the Adult dataset, we have limited the consequence of the rules to be either Income > 50K or Income =<50K. The initial proportion of this target data is unbalanced, making the target data for Adult dataset consist of an infrequent target value (rare target data).

Firstly, we apply the minimum support approach based on the initial proportion of training and test data. Next, we show the results when we have balanced the training dataset, so that we can have a similar proportion between the training and testing data. Then, we made some replication of records in the training dataset. This replication process has generated additional records for training data so that any value from the set of target values has a more similar frequency of occurrence in the training dataset and this will represent a similar proportion between each target item. Finally, we gen-erated the rules based on relative support approach proposed by [8]. Based on results obtained, we conclude that, for a rare target data, the most suitable approach in gene-rating the rules are by applying the relative support. This agrees with [8], which have successfully applied the relative support in identifying the strong co-relation of significant rare data items compared to classical minimum support approach. While the work presented in [8] purposely aims for the efficiency of rare item rule generation, our proposed framework, demonstrated its capabilities in ascertaining the generated rules. Table 3 shows the rules obtained for Iris and Wine dataset as in these datasets contained balanced target values (unified target data).

Table 3. Rules accuracy for Iris and Wine data.

Dataset Name	Dataset Description	Rule #	Type of Statistical Analysis	Accuracy	
				Training	Testing
Iris	Training : 90 records	52	Initial Rules	92.86%	90.99%
	Testing : 60 records	22	Redundancy Check	88.15%	85.29%
Wine	Training : 107 records	195	Initial Rules	87.53%	79.44%
	Testing : 71 records	17	Statistical Analysis	85.07%	81.98%
		16	Redundancy Check	85.07%	81.98%

4.4   Overall Framework Performance

Taking in the whole dataset as input would produce a large number of rules, many of which are caused by the presence of irrelevant attributes. Since the ST has more advantageous assets in comparison to MI, ST feature selection criterion is used earlier in the process to remove any irrelevant attributes. This would prevent the generation of rules that comprise of some irrelevant attributes. Hence in this experiment it is not necessary to use ST to further verify the rules as the rules were created from the attribute subset considered as relevant by the measure, as was done in [6, 13]. The attributes were ranked according to their decreasing ST and a relevance cut-off point was picked. In this experiment, the cut off value was picked based on the significant difference between the ST values in decreasing order. The significant difference was considered to occur in the ranking at the position where that attribute's ST value is less than half of the previous attribute's ST value in the ranking. At this point and below in the ranking, all attributes are considered as irrelevant, as is indicated in Table 1. For example, for Adult dataset, the relevance cutoff value is 0.0166. This is due to the ST value of attribute 'Hours Per Week' being more than double of the ST value for attribute 'Work Class'. Thus, the subset of data consists now of 10 attributes: Marital Status, Relationship, Capital Gain, Education Number, Education, Sex , Occupation, Age, Capital Loss and Hours Per Week. We proceed with the application of an association rule mining algorithm and verification of the extracted rules through statistical analysis. As discussed in 4.3, we concluded that relative support approach is capable of generating rules form a rare target data as in the Adult dataset. On the right hand side of Table 2, we show the progressive difference in the number of rules generated as statistical analysis and redundancy checks are being utilized. The combination of statistical significance analysis and redundant analysis provided proper ways in discarding non-significant rules, which is a significant reduction in the overall complexity of the rule set. From Table 2 we can also see that this great reduction of rules was not at a cost of a significant reduction in accuracy.

In Table 2, based on the statistical and redundant rules analysis performed at rules obtained from relative support approach, we managed to get 42+4 rules as our final significance rules. Input variables namely Marital Status, Relationship, Education, Sex, Occupation, Age, Capital Loss and Hours per Week are selected for the final rules. As depicted in Table 3, the result for Iris and Wine dataset also show no significant deterioration in accuracy with the reduced rule set. As to gauge the effect of rules accuracy on difference set of partitioning for each dataset, k-fold cross validation approach has being utilized, to ensure that we obtained relatively low bias and variance [1]. Based on the experimental results, we have found that the average reduction in the accuracy of the rules set is minor in comparison to the major reduction in the complexity of the rule set.

5   Conclusions and Future Works

This paper has presented a framework to ascertain the quality of the rules discovered from association rule mining which has a huge amount of rules and complex attributes measurement levels with an integrated statistical and heuristic measurement technique. The experimental results show that, this framework managed to reduce a large number of non-significant and redundant rules while at the same time relatively high accuracy was preserved. This indicates the potential of the framework in providing significant rules when applied to the structured or relational data. As part of our ongoing works, we intend to use the proposed framework to ascertain more complex rules which are discovered from semi-structured data.

References

1. Han, J., Kamber, M.: Data mining : concepts and techniques. Morgan Kaufmann Publishers, San Francisco (2001)
2. McGarry, K.: A survey of interestingness measures for knowledge discovery. Knowl. Eng. Rev. **20**, 39–61 (2005)
3. Geng, L., Hamilton, H.J.: Interestingness measures for data mining: A survey. ACM Comput. Surv. **38**, 9 (2006)
4. Zhang, H., Padmanabhan, B., Tuzhilin, A.: On the discovery of significant statistical quantitative rules. In: Proceedings of the 10th ACM SIGKDD International Conference On Knowledge Discovery And Data Mining. ACM, New York (2004)
5. Agrawal, R., Imieliski, T., Swami, A.: Mining association rules between sets of items in large databases. In: SIGMOD Rec., vol. 22, pp. 207–216 (1993)
6. Shaharanee, I.N.M., Hadzic, F., Dillon, T.S.: Interestingness of association rules using symmetrical tau and logistic regression. In: Nicholson, A., Li, X. (eds.) AI 2009. LNCS, vol. 5866, pp. 422–431. Springer, Heidelberg (2009)
7. Bing, L., Wynne, H., Yiming, M.: Mining association rules with multiple minimum supports. In: Proceedings of the 5th ACM SIGKDD International Conference on Knowledge Discovery and Data Mining. ACM, California (1999)
8. Yun, H., Ha, D., Hwang, B.: Ho Ryu, K.: Mining association rules on significant rare data using relative support. Journal of Systems and Software **67**, 181–191 (2003)

9. Tan, P.N., Kumar, V., Srivastava, J.: Selecting the right interestingness measure for association patterns. In: Proceedings of the 8th ACM SIGKDD International Conference on Knowledge Discovery and Data Mining. ACM, Alberta (2002)
10. Webb, G.I.: Discovering Significant Patterns. Machine Learning, 1–33 (2007)
11. Goodman, A., Kamath, C., Kumar, V.: Data Analysis in the 21st Century. Stat. Anal. Data Min. 1, 1–3 (2008)
12. Aumann, Y., Lindell, Y.: A Statistical Theory for Quantitative Association Rules. J. Intell. Inf. Syst. 20, 255–283 (2003)
13. Shaharanee, I.N.M., Dillon, T.S., Hadzic, F.: Ascertaining association rules using statistical analysis. In: Proceeding of the 2009 International Symposium on Computing, Communication and Control, Singapore (2009)
14. Philippe, L., Patrick, M., Benoît, V., Stéphane, L.: On selecting interestingness measures for association rules: User oriented description and multiple criteria decision aid. European Journal of Operational Research 184, 610–626 (2008)
15. Aggarwal, C.C., Yu, P.S.: A new framework for itemset generation. In: Book a new framework for itemset generation. Series A new framework for itemset generation. ACM, New York (1998)
16. Toivonen, H.: Sampling large databases for association rules. In: Proceedings of the 22th International Conference on Very Large Data Bases. Morgan Kaufmann Publishers Inc. (1996)
17. Lavrač, N., Flach, P.A., Zupan, B.: Rule evaluation measures: a unifying view. In: Džeroski, S., Flach, P.A. (eds.) ILP 1999. LNCS (LNAI), vol. 1634, pp. 174–185. Springer, Heidelberg (1999)
18. Cheng, H., Yan, X., Han, J., S., Y.P.: Direct discriminative pattern mining for effective classification. In: Proceedings of the 24th International Conference on Data Engineering, ICDE 2008, pp. 169–178 (2008)
19. Zhou, X.J., Dillon, T.S.: A statistical-heuristic feature selection criterion for decision tree induction. IEEE Transaction on Pattern Analysis and Machine Intelligence 13 (1991)
20. Julien, B., Fabrice, G., Regis, G., Henri, B.: Using information-theoretic measures to assess association rule interestingness. In: Proceedings of the 5th IEEE International Conference on Data Mining. IEEE Computer Society (2005)
21. Lotfi, S., Sadreddini, M.H.: Mining fuzzy association rules using mutual information. In: International MultiConference of Engineers and Computer Scientists, vol. 1, Hong Kong (2009)
22. Agresti, A.: An Intro to Categorical Data Analysis. Wiley-Interscience, New York (2007)
23. Hosmer, D.W., Lemeshow, S.: Applied logistic regression. Wiley, New York (1989)
24. Dillon, T.S., Hossain, T., Bloomer, W., Witten, M.: Improvements in supervised BRAINNE: a method for symbolic data mining using neural networks. In: Seventh Conference on Database Semantics, vol. 124, pp. 67–88. Chapman & Hall, Switzerland (1998)
25. Shaharanee, I., Hadzic, F.: Evaluation and optimization of frequent, closed and maximal association rule based classification. Stat. Comput. 23, 1–23 (2013)
26. Shaharanee, I., Hadzic, F., Dillon, T.: Interestingness measures for association rules based on statistical validity. Knowl.-Based Syst. 24(3), 386–392 (2011)

Rule-Based Multi-criteria Framework
for SaaS Application Architecture Selection

Falak Nawaz[1(✉)], Ahmad Mohsin[1], Syda Fatima[1], and Naeem Khalid Janjua[2]

[1] Department of Computer Science and Engineering, Air University, Multan, Pakistan
`{fnn,ahmad,fatima}@aumc.edu.pk`
[2] School of Business, University of New South Wales, Canberra, Australia
`n.janjua@unsw.edu.au`

Abstract. Software-as-a-service (SaaS) is a very successful model for providing cloud-based services over the internet. However, due to the dynamic nature of SaaS services, it becomes very challenging to ensure provision of scalability, applying frequent maintenance and functionality updates to SaaS Services. SOAP and REST are the two mostly used software architectural styles for accessing and consuming SaaS services in cloud environment and each have its distinct advantages. Therefore, to address above mentioned challenges, it is critical to choose the suitable architectural style because the success of a SaaS is strongly coupled with its architecture style. Choosing the right software architecture for a system is a multi-criteria decision making problem and it takes into consideration the architectural style characteristics, non-functional requirements and working domain requirements. In this paper, we propose a rule-based multi-criteria decision support system (DSS) for a SaaS application architecture selection. Our proposed DSS uses weighted sum model (WSM) that take into account the architectural style characteristics, non-functional and domain specific requirements.

Keywords: Cloud computing · Software as a service · Software architecture · SOA · REST · SOAP · Architectural style · Decision support system

1   Introduction

Cloud computing provides ubiquitous access to shared pool of configurable computing resources, software and data services hosted over the internet. The five important characteristics of cloud computing model are on-demand self-service, broad network access, resource pooling, rapid elasticity and measured service [2]. The cloud computing service models are software-as-a-service (SaaS), infrastructure-as-a-service (IaaS), and platform-as-a-service (PaaS).

Cloud computing is built on top of virtualization that consists of compute, storage and network components in servers. Virtualization provides a solid foundation for cloud computing to expand. However, cloud computing service models are not mature enough. These service models require proven software design and architecture in order to provide scalable cloud computing platforms [4]. Therefore, selecting a suitable architecture for SaaS service provisioning is a critical decision and it contributes

© IFIP International Federation for Information Processing 2015
T. Dillon (Ed.): IFIP AI 2015, IFIP AICT 465, pp. 129–138, 2015.
DOI: 10.1007/978-3-319-25261-2_12

towards success of the software. Software architecture describes the complete design of any system. This includes identifying system components, their interactions, granularity of communication needed for interactions, placement of system components in different subsystems, and interface protocols used for communication. Hence, selection of the correct software architecture is critical for the successful implementation of cloud computing platform.

In literature, different architectural styles have been used for delivery of service over the Internet. Service-oriented Architecture (SOA), in broader context, is an evolution of software architecture that provides software application functionality as a service to other applications or services. SOA provides software architectural guidelines for non-functional requirements such as reusability, modularity, extensibility and flexibility. Cloud computing platforms have not fully adopted SOA to make them more reusable, flexible and extensible [3]. To build scalable cloud computing platform, we need to leverage SOA to build reusable components, standardized interfaces, and extensible solution.

A Web service provides basic building block to develop a SOA based application. Web service is a method of communications between two computers over a network. There are two very famous types of web service architectural styles that are SOAP and REST. SOAP based implementations are also termed as Service oriented Architecture (SOA) while REST based implementations are known as Resource Oriented Architecture (ROA). We will explore these two architectural styles in next section.

Due to the complexity of cloud computing environment and the software systems running on it, success of the system strongly depends on their architecture. Software architecture has been a key element in software development process for last two decades [14]. Moreover, software architecture selection is a multi-criteria decision-making problem in which software architect try to analyze different goals and objectives for the system under consideration. Some architectural styles may have good effects on a particular problem domain but may not be suitable for another problem domain. Similarly, both REST and SOAP have their own quality attributes and limitations that may have good or bad effect(s) on different problem domains. Although comprehensive list of attributes have been listed for each style in different texts, but we cannot understand the extent to what advantages and disadvantages of quality and quantity attributes of architecture are considered [14]. Therefore, comparing capabilities, characteristics and benefits of software architecture is somehow difficult task. In this paper, a rule based decision support system (DSS) has been developed which tries to support the decision making process by considering different related criteria for web service architecture including quality attributes, domain requirements and architectural style characteristics.

In the next section, a comparison of REST and SOAP architectural styles is presented. In Section 3 we will describe the motivation for selection of architectural style in cloud-based environment. Section 4 will present factors and criteria for architectural styles, non-functional requirements and domain requirements for multi-criteria decision making. Section 5 will present proposed DSS for Web service architectural selection and finally Section 6 will conclude this paper.

2   REST vs. SOAP

A Web service provides software functionality online that is accessible through network endpoints. As discussed above, Web service can be technically distinguished between SOAP and RESTful Web services.

SOAP Web services use XML for message format and description of interfaces (WSDL). A SOAP-based architectural style is suitable for application domain with following characteristics [5].

- A formal contract is required between service provider and consumer. Web Services Description Language (WSDL) takes care of all the information required about the web service operations, parameters, types and message format. This is useful in situations where service composition is required in complex business process models.
- Architecture needs to handle complex non-functional requirements such as security, trust and coordination.
- Architecture needs to handle asynchronous invocation and processing of service requests.

RESTful web services are usually considered suitable for lightweight and ad hoc services. RESTful web services use existing W3C standards, e.g. HTTP. A REST-based architectural style is suitable for application domain with following characteristics.

- There is no formal description of service endpoints (e.g. no WSDL) between service producer and consumer. The service producers usually provide some additional toolkits describing how to invoke REST web services.
- Architecture needs to handle non-functional requirements such as scalability, network bandwidth, and integration.
- Architectures where web services are completely stateless just like HTTP requests on a website. For example, existing web applications can expose their functionality easily through CRUD operations using RESTful web services.

Many comparative studies have been carried out to identify strengths and weaknesses of SOAP and RESTful Web services with respect to architecture, technology, security, performance, and scalability. The conceptual, principal and technological level comparison of RESTful Web services and SOAP based "big" web services is performed in [6]. The author says, "On the principle level, two approaches have similar quantitative characteristics. On the conceptual level, less architectural decisions must be made when deciding for SOAP-based Web services. On the technology level, the same number of decisions must be made but fewer alternatives have to be considered when building RESTful Web services". SOAP-based Web services produce considerable network traffic and high latency due to large message size [8]. But payload size in SOAP can be reduced using different compression techniques [7]. RESTful Web services have better performance than SOAP-based Web services in wired and wireless communication networks. The RESTful web services are lightweight, easy and self-descriptive with higher flexibility and lower overhead.

Another main difference between REST and SOAP Web services [9] is that SOAP is a tightly coupled design similar to RPC (Remote Procedure Call), and REST is a loosely coupled design similar to navigating Web links. As a study of two opposing standards based on SOAP and REST, SOAP has the advantage of tight coupling of operations, while REST has the advantage of scalability and lightweight access to its operations. REST has the disadvantage of managing the name space with a large number of objects, and a disadvantage of SOAP is the need for dedicated client ports for different types of notification. REST principles also played an important role in standardizing SOAP 1.2.

Internet of Things (IoTs) and Mobile devices has taken this discussion of selecting REST or SOAP style architecture to the next level. A comparative study of SOAP vs REST for provisioning Web services on Mobile phone is performed in [7]. A benchmarking evaluation of SOAP and RESTful Web services is performed in [10] for mobile devices. Benchmarking includes string concatenation and float number addition web services. The performance evaluation results show the advantages of using RESTful web services over conventional web services for mobile devices. Authors in [11] compared REST and SOAP Web services with respect to performance. They concluded that RESTful Web services are now emerging as an alternative to SOAP-based Web services and might be a more suitable choice in some cases.

The more recent work on SOAP and REST highlights that Web Service performance is becoming an important factor. This work "concluded that RESTful web service is a better alternative for SOAP based web services. SOAP based web services are produces considerable network traffic, high latency and the message size is also large this is not in the case of RESTful. The RESTful web services have better performance than SOAP based web services in wired and wireless communication network. The RESTful web services are lightweight, easy and self-descriptive with higher flexibility and lower overhead [12].

3   Motivation

Evolution of Cloud services, Internet of Things (IoTs) and Web mobile apps are shaping the future of internet. This will determine how smartphones and physical devices will interact with each other. In this paper, we have focused on why choosing the right architecture for cloud based software-as-a-service (SaaS) is important and what factors drive architecture selection.

Each architectural style chosen has trade-offs related to Non-functional requirements (NFRs) and Architectural characteristics (ACs). Domain requirements (DRs) are equally important while choosing the right architecture. Currently software architect give less preference to the domain requirements while choosing the architecture. Within each of above mentioned area, there are number factors that need to be taken care of while choosing the right architecture. But there is no such automated tool that makes this multi-criteria decision making easy. Very rare work has been done in this domain. Existing systems focus on ACs and DRs only [14] and does not take NFRs into account. Our proposed DSS takes all three areas into consideration and uses a knowledge base that has the ability to update its knowledge and suggest suitable choices to the software architect.

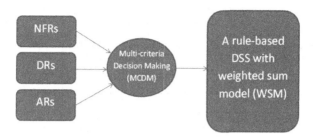

Fig. 1. Pictorial representation of the problem

Architecture must be chosen according to the nature of the applications, its domain requirements, non-functional requirements and required characteristics of architecture. Architecture style chosen by considering these requirements will be best suited for cloud based software-as-a-services (SaaS). Therefore a need for decision support systems in this domain is appreciated.

4   Multi-criteria Decision Maker for Architecture Selection

A multi-criteria decision maker will give suitable option to software architect for solving above mentioned problem. A decision support system (DSS) provides support for all phases of the decision making process. It should be easy to use meanwhile providing support for users at all levels to make decision [14]. We have used CLIPS as a Rule-Based DSS in which the knowledge component includes procedural and inferential rules. We found number of ACs and NFRs for various domains and tried to analyze cloud based SaaS web services. We then prepared a comparative analysis of these ACs and NFRs for both SOAP and REST implementations.

4.1   Domain Requirements (DRs)

We have selected some domain characteristics (or high level functional requirements) according to type of application. The selected cloud-based SaaS web services fall in the following domains: E-commerce, Logistics, Telecommunications and Health-care.

4.2   Architectural Characteristics (ACs)

We explored the architectural characteristics for SOAP and REST that important for selection of architecture. The characteristics that are considered in our DSS are given below in Table 1.

Table 1. Architectural Characteristics

Architectural Style Characteris-	SOA	REST
Heterogeneity	✓	✓
Protocol layering	✓	✓
Loose coupling	✓	✓
Integration style	✓	✓
Resource identification	✗	✓
URI design	✗	✓
Resource interaction semantic	✗	✓
Resource relationship	✗	✓
Contract design	✓	✓
Data representation	✓	✓
Message exchange pattern	✓	✓
Traffic monitoring	✗	✗
Traffic determination	✗	✗
Traffic transformation	✗	✗
Service description	✓	✓
Service identification	✓	✓
Service composition	✓	✓

4.3   Non-Functional Requirements (NFRs)

There are a number of non-functional requirements and their sub-factors but we only selected security, reliability and performance as key NFRs for our DSS for architecture selection process. The reason for selecting these NFRs is that these are the most common NFRs required for applications domains mentioned above.

Table 2. Common NFRs required for applications domains

NFR	Sub-factors	SOAP	REST
Security	Encryption	✓	✓
	Integrity	✓	✓
	Authentication	✓	✓
	Authorization	✓	✓
	Non-repudiation	✓	✓
	Confidentiality	✓	✓

Table 2. (*Continued*)

Reliability	Point-to-Point	✓	✓
	Ordered delivery of message	✓	✓
	Delivery status	✓	✓
	Elimination of duplicate message	✓	✓
	Resending message	✓	✗
	Reliable delivery of message	✓	✓
Performance	Caching	✗	✓
	Load balancing	✗	✓
	Throughput	✓	✓
	Response time	✓	✓
	Latency	✓	✓
	Execution time	✓	✓

5   Working of Proposed Rule-Based DSS

In order to select architecture style correctly and precisely, all existing information related to the application are considered. The proposed DSS uses characteristics of Web service architectural styles, characteristics of domain of application being developed and non-functional requirements. We assigned weightage to these characteristics and requirements against both REST and SOAP architectures and used this weighted criteria for inference in DSS. The complete design of proposed DSS is depicted in figure 2 in detail. The proposed DSS has five essential components that help in decision making process.

- Repository
- Tools
- Rule base
- Decision maker
- User interface

Responsibilities of each component and what they contribute to decision making process is given below.

5.1   Repository

We have three types of repositories which are DRs (Domain Requirements), NFRs (Non-Functional Requirements) and ACs (Architecture Characteristics). In DRs we have characteristics regarding requirements for different domains mentioned in the previous section. NFRs contain requirements provided by different quality attributes and also information regarding the number of sub-attributes of quality attributes provided by specific web service architectural style. ACs has information of all the characteristics of web service architectural styles SOAP and REST so that architect can select according to the nature of application being developed.

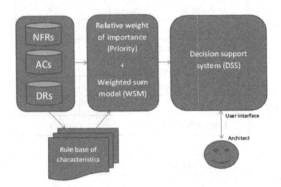

Fig. 2. Rule-based DSS for Web service architectural style selection

5.2   Tools

Domain requirements and architectural styles characteristics would be prioritized on the basis of number of characteristics selected.

When the necessary information is gathered and importance of levels of quality attributes are obtained, the DSS applies Weighted Sum Model (WSM) for NFRs and number of characteristics required for specific Web service architectural style and domain requirements would already be counted while gathering information according to the need of app being developed as shown in figure 2. WSM is the simplest MCDA (multi-criteria decision analysis/making) method for calculating a single result from a number of alternatives [15].

We can generalize an MCDA problem by assuming M alternatives and N decision criteria [16]. We further assume that all criteria/factors mentioned in Table 1 and Table 2 are our benefit criteria which means that higher the values, the better it is. A tick mark in the table is assumed to have a value of 1 and cross mark is assigned 0. Next suppose that w_j denotes the relative weight of importance (priority) of the criterion c_j and a_{ij} is the performance value of alternative A_i when it is evaluated in terms of criterion c_j. Then, the total (i.e., when all the criteria are considered simultaneously) importance of alternative A_i, denoted as $A_i^{WSM\text{-}score}$, is defined as follows:

$$A_i^{WSM\text{-}Score} = \sum_{j=1} w_j \, a_{ij}, \text{ for } i = 1, 2, \ldots, m$$

In this case, SOAP and REST are alternatives and quality attributes (such as security, reliability, performance) and architectural style characteristics are criteria. The rules that are extracted from architecture characteristics, Non-functional requirements, domain requirements and the priorities as defined by the user of the DSS will become inputs to the system.

5.3   Rule Base

In order to make decisions, we need some rules which indicate the interaction among DRs, NFRs and ACs with respect to the nature of Web services being developed. In other words, the rules determine which domain characteristics are required, which characteristics of architecture are required, what is the importance level of each quality attribute. These rules are kept in the rule base and are extracted from repository.

5.4   Decision Maker

Decision maker provides a rule-based engine to allow a wide range of knowledge to be represented as heuristics or rule of thumb. These rules specify a set of actions to be performed for a given situation. This component is responsible of receiving information about the priorities c_i of every domain requirements, architecture characteristics and non-functional requirements from software architect via user interface. These priorities c_i are considered as inputs for the weighted sum model for NFRs and ACs, the decision maker determines a particular architectural style suitable for the cloud-based services being developed. This result is then displayed to the user through user interface. If there is more than one architectural style suitable for a particular domain, the system recommends all of them, leaving the final choice to the software architect. The system also has the learning capability of storing the final selected architecture by the architect in knowledge base and uses it in future for similar situations to recommend right architecture.

5.5   User Interface

The user interface is responsible for receiving the information from user regarding domain requirements, architectural style characteristics, non-functional requirements and also the priorities for NFRs and ACs. The suggested architecture style(s) is/are represented by user interface as a suggestion to the architect by their priority.

6   Conclusion

REST and SOAP are the most used architectural styles for implementing cloud-based software-as-a-services (SaaS). Due to complexity, frequent maintenance and updates of the implemented services, it is important to choose the right architectural style based on NFRs, architectural style characteristics and domain requirements. However, choosing the right architectural style is a multi-criteria decision making problem that requires all the factors to be considered along with their priorities by the software architect. Our proposed system solves this problem by using the weighted sum model (WSM) and rule-based DSS. By defining ACs and NFRs criteria in the form of rules and using relative weight of importance (priority) to WSM, we get a suggested architectural style that is suitable for the given domain.

References

1. Fielding, R.T.: Architectural Styles and the Design of Network-based Software Architectures. Doctoral dissertation, Dept. of Information and Computer Science, Univ. of California, Irvine (2000)
2. Mell, P., Grance, T.: The NIST definition of Cloud Computing. NIST, Gaithersburg (2011). Special Publication 800-145
3. Zhang, L.J., Zhou, Q.: CCOA: cloud computing open architecture. In: The Proceedings of IEEE International Conference of Web Services (2009)
4. Zhang, A.B., Su, L., Sun, Y., Lu, M.: Research on cloud computing technology serving space TT&C applications. In: Proceedings of the 27th Conference of Spacecraft TT&C Technology. Lecture Notes in Electrical Engineering, Guangzhou (2015)
5. http://docs.oracle.com/javaee/6/tutorial/doc/giqsx.html
6. Pautasso, C., Zimmeraman, O., Leyman, F.: RESTful web services vs. "Big" web services: making the right architectural decision. In: WWW 2008, Beijing, April 21–25, 2008
7. Wagh, K., Thool, R.: A Comparative Study of SOAP Vs REST Web Services Provisioning Techniques for Mobile Host. Journal of Information Engineering and Applications (2012)
8. Mumbaikar, S., Padiya, P.: Web Services Based On SOAP and REST Principles. International Journal of Scientific and Research Publications 3(5) (May 2013)
9. Muehlen, M.Z., Nickerson, J.V., Swenson, K.D.: Developing Web Services Choreography Standards - The Case of REST vs. SOAP. Elsevier B.V. (2004)
10. Hamad, H., Saad, M., Abed, R.: Performance Evaluation of RESTful Web Services for Mobile Devices. Computer Engineering Department, Islamic University of Gaza, Palestine International Arab Journal of e-Technology 1(3) (January 2010)
11. Belqasmi, F., Singh, J., Melhem, S.Y.B., Glitho, R.H.: SOAP-Based vs. RESTful Web Services: A Case Study for Multimedia Conferencing. IEEE Internet Computing 16(4), 54–63 (2012). doi:10.1109/MIC.2012
12. Guinard, D.: A Web of Things Application Architecture - Integrating the Real-world into the Web. Ph.D. thesis No. 19891, ETH Zurich, Zurich, Switzerland, August 2011
13. Moaven, S., Habibi, J., Ahmadi, H., Kamandi, A.: A decision support system for software architecture-style selection. In: Sixth International Conference on Software Engineering Research, Management and Application (2008)
14. Triantaphyllou, E.: Multi-Criteria Decision Making: A Comparative Study, p. 320. Kluwer Academic Publishers (now Springer), Dordrecht (2000). ISBN 0-7923-6607-7
15. Nawaz, F., Qadir, K., Farooq Ahmad, H.: SEMREG-Pro: a semantic based registry for proactive web service discovery using publish subscribe model. In: The Fourth International Conference on Semantics, Knowledge and Grid. IEEE, China (2008)
16. Svahnberg, M.: Supporting Software Architecture Evolution - Architecture Selection and Variability. Ph.D. Thesis, Blekinge Institute of Technology (2003)
17. Janjua, N.K., et al.: Digital health care ecosystem: SOA compliant HL7 based health care information interchange. In: 3rd IEEE Internationals Conference on Digital Ecosystems and Technologies, DEST 2009. IEEE (2009)

Interleaving Collaborative Planning and Execution Along with Deliberation in Logistics and Supply Chain

Naeem Khalid Janjua, Omar Khadeer Hussain$^{(\boxtimes)}$, and Elizabeth Chang

School of Business, Australian Defence Force Academy, University of New South Wales,
Canberra, Australia
{n.janjua,o.hussain,e.chang}@adfa.edu.au

Abstract. Automated planning is a rich technical filed in Artificial Intelligence (AI) and most of the existing research focused on path finding methods in a compact state-transition system where planning is decoupled from execution. The introduction of the Web has led to increasing emphasis in AI on the development of planning algorithms for real-world applications where planning is distributed and plan generation can happen concurrently with plan execution. An example of one such real-world application is logistics and supply chain. In this paper, we envisage a collaborative planning and execution framework for logistics and supply chain operations. The framework supports human planners for a collaborative plan construction. The planning is interleaved with execution where new information collected during execution is used to refine the plan if required. Additionally, planning is defeasible in nature. During planning either conflicting viewpoints may arise among planners and/or the new information collected during execution may result in conflicts among planned tasks (situations). Deliberation module in the proposed framework provides a platform to human planners where they can start an argumentative dialogue to resolve the conflicts by establishing preferences between conflicting tasks. We use situation calculus to model the framework and propose an algorithm to interleave collaborative planning with execution along with deliberation support.

1 Introduction

Planning and decision making processes have been a hot research area in AI for decades with applications in various domains. For example, it is a core activity to the design, organisation and control of logistics and supply chain activities such as procurement, transportation, inventory management, warehousing and materials handling, quality of services, information management and sharing, risk management etc. Collaborative planning is a process of decision making among interdependent parities that involves joint ownership of decisions and collective responsibility of outcomes, and work as coalitions to achieve common goals that otherwise would have been impossible or too expensive to achieve by an individual party. It is a method for solving shared problems by resolving conflicts.

Collaborative planning consists of two important phases, namely; planning and execution. Traditionally, these were separate apart. Most of the planning systems research

© IFIP International Federation for Information Processing 2015
T. Dillon (Ed.): IFIP AI 2015, IFIP AICT 465, pp. 139–148, 2015.
DOI: 10.1007/978-3-319-25261-2_13

focused on automated path finding methods in a compact, state-transition system and they ignored the human aspect in decision making process. These systems as categorised as an offline planning system. For example, in logistics and supply chain it is well-known that the strength of transactional enterprise resource planning (ERP) systems is not in the area of planning instead its execution. Hence, Advanced Planning Systems (APS) have been developed to fill this gap. APS are based on the principles of hierarchical planning and make extensive use of solution approaches known as mathematical programming and meta-heuristics.

Multi-agent system planning systems are APS systems applied to independent or loosely-coupled problems to enhance the benefit of distributed planning between autonomous agents as solving this type of problem requires less coordination [19]. Most of automated software agents who engage in collaboration with others, build a model of other agents' mental states and update their own beliefs and goals as the dialogue progresses. This process is known as dialogue understanding [6]. To handle uncertainty, argumentation-driven frameworks have been proposed that allows different users to share their knowledge and resolve conflicts between them to reach the common goal have been proposed in the literature [19]. However, in most MAP systems, planning provides the solution, and on execution part, it is executed as merely traversing the identified path. Such system work well in close world assumption where all of the possible effects of each action are know in advance. However, planning becomes very challenging if the environment is dynamically changing (open world assumptions) and is not pre-engineered to conform to software agent needs. Additionally, automated agents might not able to interpret human planner's intensions and could lack ability of planning and deliberation under uncertainty.

The introduction of WWW has led to increasing emphasis in AI on development of planning algorithms for real-world applications where planning is distributed and plan generation can happen concurrently with plan execution. When and how to interleave planning and execution is well defined complex problem in the literature [18]. Additionally, the challenges for software tools supporting collaborative planning include master data integration, user-specific secure data access and the mutual decision-making process. Systems that enable collaborative planning must support partners during each step of the process [11]. The introduction of Semantic Web technology tools for collaboration has addressed some of the issues of collaborative programming such as information has meaning attached to it that makes it understandable across organisational boundaries. The Collaborative planning and acting model [16] is the first attempt that supports human planners in managing, planning information and facilitates the planning process with automated reasoning. However, currents Semantic Web based Collaborative planning models lack the means of representation incomplete, contradictory information and logical relations that define constraints and axioms of domain begin modeled [14].

In our previous work [8], we proposed a framework for incomplete and conflicting information representation and developed argumentation-based algorithms for reasoning over such information in Semantic Web applications. In this paper, we extend our previous work and apply it in the area of logistics and supply chain where planning for operational risk may need to be addressed at a spoke by considering the information from other multiple global and region specific locations. We propose a conceptual framework and develop algorithms that interleave planning and execution, thus allow in a timely manner enables the human planners to plan and execute the tasks. In case of conflicting viewpoints, planners start an argumentative dialogue to resolve the conflicts, integrate the changes in the plan and proceed with the execution. We use situation calculus to model the the framework and Defeasible Logic Programming (DeLP) for knowledge representation and reasoning in logistics operations.

2   Related Work

This work lies at the intersection of Artificial intelligence, in particular classical and distributed planning, Multi agent systems, Argumentation based dialogue systems, Reasoning about actions and change, and the Semantic Web. Automated planning system is a kind of APS system that has been an endeavour of AI leading to nmerous technologies, however, their application in real world applications has been unfortunately relatively low [7, 16].

Multi-agent planning system (MAP) involves several autonomous software agents in planning or plan execution activity, share their knowledge and capabilities to provide solutions to loosely-coupled problems with minimum coordination [4]. Collaborative planning is a distributed planning which as been an active area of research in AI for decades and it is still an open challenge. The various existing work on MAP approaches can be classified according to the planning and coordination models they use.

Firstly, **pre-planning distribution of tasks** where a software agent plans and distributes the tasks to other agents. For example, Multi-agent Planning by plan Reuse (MARP) agent allocates the task goals to the participating agents that consider both private and public information. MARP agent then calls each agent iteratively for a solution [2]. In another work [3] agent automatically decomposes tasks into MAP problems, which are then locally solved through a centralized heuristic planner. Emphasis is pre-planning for task distribution and execution by individual agents.

Secondly, **planning followed by merging plan through coordination** where software agents construct independent plans for different subgoals and a centralized algorithm is used to merge those plans. The emphasis is on problem of controlling and coordinating a local plan of agents. For example [5] of the most well known approach for coordination of plans called as a partial global planning framework. Planning First is one of the first planners where agents individually synthesize plans through a state-based planner and the resulting local plans are then coordinated through a distributed Constraint Satisfaction Problem [15].

Thirdly, **interleaving planning and coordination** where software agents propose an iterative refinement of the base plan until a consistent joint plan is obtained that solves the problem. Several advantages of this approach have been discussed in the literature [19].

Although APS systems discussed above provide promising solutions, however, they lack implementations in real world scenarios such as logistics and supply chain. The various reasons reported in literature that leads to low penetration of above mentioned APS systems in real world application areas are as follows [7, 16]:

1. Human planners want to use tool for better visibility of the planning process but want to control the decision making part of planning phase.
2. High level of automation results in reduced situation awareness, complex and skill degradation.
3. The huge amount time and manpower needed to enter all information.
4. Difficulty of converting human concepts into tool supported language.

Therefore, this research is an attempt to overcome the limitations of the APS system identified above. We propose a conceptual framework to support planning interleaving with execution along with deliberation to help the human planners in determining which actions are possible at current stage, helping them in making the best choice by building arguments in favour and against conflicting planning tasks, refine the plan and execute it.

3   Basic Action Theory

Our formalization model is based on situation calculus [13]. We describe and employ the extended version of Reiter [17] to formalization our model for argumentation-based collaborative planning and acting model.

In our model, each human planner maintains the representation of the domain as basic action theory and it has the following form:

$$\mathcal{D} = \Sigma \cup \mathcal{D}_{ss} \cup \mathcal{D}_{ap} \cup \mathcal{D}_{una} \cup \mathcal{D}_{S0} \tag{1}$$

Where

- Σ is a set of fundamental domain-independent axioms providing the basic properties of the situation.
- $\mathcal{D}_{ss}$ is a set of successor state axioms represent relational or functional fluents in the domain. Formally, $Poss(a, s) \supset [T (do(a, s)) \equiv \gamma_T^+ (a, s) \vee (T (s) \wedge \neg\gamma_T^+ (a, s))]$ where γ_T^+ and γ_T^- represent the add and delete conditions of fluent T.
- $\mathcal{D}_{ap}$ is a set of precondition axioms under which action can be performed. Formally, represented as $\Pi_A (s) \equiv Poss(A, S)$.
- $\mathcal{D}_{una}$ is a set of unique names axioms for actions.
- $\mathcal{D}_{S0}$ is a set of first order sentence that represents initial state of the world.

A basic action theory for logistics application specifies a plan and the tasks of the domain of concern and the contextual settings in which the dialogue operates. A plan in situation calculus is treated as an executable situation that satisfies a goal statement. We assume that the sets Fluents, NonFluents and Actions are shared among the planners. Additionally, they share a common goal, knowledge about the fundamental axioms, unique name axioms for actions and the names of object in the domain. We use the definition of plan and planning problem defined in [1] as follows:

Definition 1. *Given a basic action theory D and a Goal g with single free variable s, a plan π is a variable-free situation term s_π iff $D| = executable(s_\pi) \wedge g(s_\pi)$ where executable $(s_\pi) \stackrel{def}{=} (\forall a, s^*).do(a, s^*) \sqsubseteq s_\Pi \supset Poss(a, s^*).$*

It is important to note here is that the term s_π represents the history for the execution of the actions of a plan in sequence.

Definition 2. *A planning problem P is a tuple $< D, g >$ where D is a basic action theory denoting the planning domain and g is a fluent sentence specifying the goal.*

As a result of above definition of plan and foundational axioms for situations we can identify that $excutable(do(a, s)) \equiv executable(s) \wedge P oss(a, s)$. This enables the transformation of plan definition as follows:

Definition 3. *A plan $\pi = A_1, A_2; \ldots; A_n$ is a solution to a planning problem p iif*
$$D |= \quad Poss(A_1, S_0) \wedge do(A_1, S_0) = S_1 \wedge Poss(A_2, S_1) \wedge do(A_1, S_1) = S_2 \wedge \cdots \wedge$$
$$Poss(A_n, S_{n-1}) \wedge do(A_n, S_{n-1}) = S_n \wedge G(S_n).$$

This definition asserts that the actions in the plan can be performed in sequence eventually performing the final action results in goal sentence $\mathcal{G}$ be true.

A basic action theory is necessary to define a domain for reasoning. However, in classical AI reasoning is performed under certain assumption such as follows:

1. The given problem can be fully addressed with available information (solution to the problem lies within the available situation tree). In order to elucidate it, let us consider an example. A planner wants to improve a decision making process and he believes that all the information he holds is sufficient to identify the issues and address them.
2. The domain knowledge is consistent. In other words, they assume that there will be no conflicting events and situation during the decision-making process.
3. New information is consistent with the already available information or specifications.
4. New information does not lead to retraction of previous conclusions.

Because of these limitations discussed above, AI failed to provide a solution to many real world scenarios where some of the information or actions in a plan may result in conflicting situations. To overcome this, we employ a model based on an extended version of action theory, $\mathcal{D}_{ext}$, that consider representation of conflicts and provide support for conflict resolution dialogue methodology.

Definition 4. *Extended action theory is defined as follows:*
$$\mathcal{D}_{ext} = \mathcal{D} \cup \Omega_c \cup \Omega_p$$

where

– $\mathcal{D}$ is a basic action theory.

– Ω_c is a set of axioms for representing conflicting information. For example argument(X,p), argument(Y,$\neg p$), counterArgument(Y, X, do(a,s)), under-Cut(Z,C, do(a,l)) etc.

– Ω_p is an set of axioms used in deliberation module such as speech acts for communication and dialogue movies for establishing preference between conflicting situations. For example, propose(A), reject(A), Argue(A= >P), Why(P), Support(P) etc.

Definition 5. *A situation p conflicts with situation ¬p in a plan iff ¬p executes action a after p has executed an internal action ¬a that conflict with a in the system.*

$Conflict(a, a) = counterArgument(p, ¬p, do(a, s)) =_{def}$ $p /= ¬p \wedge P$ $oss(¬p, a, s) \wedge$
$(\exists¬a, s)[P$ $oss(p, a, s) \wedge do(a, s) \subset s \wedge P$ $oss(a, a, >, s)]$

A set of possible conflicts set $Conf{\hat{l}}ict$ contains situations that can be used to generate counter-arguments. Note that no situation weights are used in both plan construction and conflict set. Therefore, the attack between arguments are symmetric i.e. they are equally acceptable. Therefore, planners need to perform meta-argumentation to establish a preference between conflicting arguments. Therefore, *Preference (á, a)= $_{def}$ Assign(Conflict(á, a)))*, where assign is a primitive action that triggers Deliberation Dialogue.

The deliberation dialogue is a meta-argumentation system consists of union of arguments that are constructed by the proponent and the opponents i.e. $A = A_{pro}$ U A_{opps} . As a result of the dialogue process, argumentation lines are constructed and acceptability of arguments is computed to establish priority between conflicting situations. Once the priority is established, the preference is included into the plan along with reasoning/argumentation line supporting it. We reuse the syntax and semantics for argumentation system defined in [10] and extend it for dialogue based system using semantics defined in [12]. We explain the working of argumentation based dialogue system in section 4.

Definition 6. *Given extended action theory D_{ext} , a collaborative plan Π for a common Goal G is a variable-free situation term s_Π iff D_{ext} $|= executable(s_\Pi)$ $\wedge G(s_\pi)$ where*

$executable(s_\Pi) \stackrel{def}{=} (\forall a, s^*).do(a, s^*)$ $c; s_\Pi \supset P$ $oss(a, s^*)$ *and if conflict exists, there exists a preference relationship, such that $Preference(a, a) \equiv Support(a, a) |= do(a, s)$*

Definition 7. *A collaborative planning solution CP_s is a tuple $< D_{ext}, G, \hat{p} >$ where D_{ext} is extended action theory for representing the sequence of actions and G is a fluent sentence specifying the goal and $\hat{p}$ represents the priority relationships over conflicting situations.*

4   Conceptual Framework

The conceptual framework shown in figure 1 provides the infrastructure for collaborative planning to synthesis plan whose success is suggested by the evidence provided by the planners and evaluate the acceptability of the plan by comparing the evidence supporting them against possible objections (conflicts). The advantage of deliberation (argumentative dialogue) within the domain of decision making is its ability to manage conflicts in the knowledge, preferences and the rules by which a decision is made.

Therefore, the notion of acceptability is embedded within the planning problem and the plans are supported with arguments. In following sub-sections we explain working of the framework in detail.

4.1 Planning Module

A planner needs to reason about its actions. Therefore, they need models for choosing, organising, and revisiting their actions and plans [7]. During collaborative planning it might be possible that planner may need to retract from planning task defined earlier. Therefore, the knowledge representation model should be expressive enough to

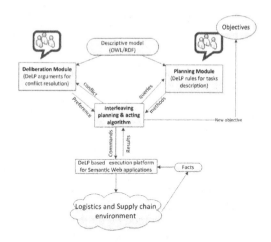

Fig. 1. Interleaving collaborative planning and execution framework along with deliberation in logistics and supply chain

represent planning task that may be retracted later. Therefore the planning is defeasible in nature.

DeLP is a general-purpose defeasible argumentation formalism based on logic programming, intended to model inconsistent and potentially contradictory knowledge (both strong and weak negation). A defeasible logic program has the form $\psi = (\Pi, \Delta)$, where Π and Δ stand for strict knowledge and defeasible knowledge, respectively. We extended DeLP for knowledge representation and reasoning in semantic web application [8].

We defined syntax and semantics for strict and defeasible rule representation. We reuse our work here for defining the planning tasks. In the rule base, a planning task (rule) takes the following form *[rule identifier] [rule body] [type of rule] [head]*. The rule body represents precondition and rule head represent the effects. Planners have objective and to achieve them, they define tasks using a web-based interface. A human planner who need to collaborate with other hu- man planners to achieve some common goals, define their planning tasks in the form of strict and defeasible rules. Each planner defines its tasks and as a result the system produces a process map using forward chain reasoning as described in [9]. In such collaborative problem solving model, forward chain reasoning is used to digitize the plans and make them alive for the human planners. For more information about forward chain reasoning using rete algorithm, readers are referred to [10]. It is important to note is that the planning task are initiated with domain knowledge defined in descriptive model. We used ontologies to de- fine domain knowledge and used rules defined in Table 1 to transform ontology implicit knowledge to become explicit for rule based reasoning.

Table 1. Translation rules for OWL/RDF predicates to DeLP facts

Rule 1	type(X,C)→C(X)	Class
Rule 2	subClassof(Sc, C), Sc(X)→C(X)	Subclass
Rule 3	objectProperty(X), domain(X, Y), range(X,Z) →X (Y, Z)	Object Property
Rule 4	objectProperty(X), X(Z, V), subProperty(X, Y)→Y(Z, X)	subProperty
Rule 5	dataProperty(X), domain(X, Y), range(X, Z) →X(Y, Z)	Data Property
Rule 6	dataproperty(X), X(Z, V), subProperty(X, Y)→Y(Z, X)	SubProperty

4.2   Deliberation Module

Time pressure and the distributed nature of logistics and supply chain, force the planners to execute an action. In non-deterministic planning domain, execution of plan tasks is the best source of collecting real observations as an effect of the plan. In most of real world applications, planning is defeasible in nature and execution of plan tasks may result in conflicting tasks or retraction of previous planning results. We build deliberation module on the work done by [12] and it helps planners firstly; to put forward their arguments that may be incomplete statements and offer them ways of advancing well-formed arguments as well as to reuse arguments that often appear in discussions, secondly; with the help of algorithms to compute the acceptability of arguments at any stage of the discussion. The deliberation module is defined by:

- Topic Language: DeLP as a logical language.
- Argumentation Logic: as defined in [10]. The only difference is that in our previous work it was assumed that system has collated all the relevant infor mation and hybrid reasoning engine reasoning over it. Here, we replace auto- mated algorithm with human planners and conflict resolution process is a dialogue driven activity. We reuse the definition of argument, subargument, attack, static defeat , dynamic defeat.
- Communication Language: Set of Locutions S and two binary relation Ra and Rs of attacking and surrendering reply on S.
- Dialogue Moves and Termination: as defined in [12].

It might be possible that task defined as defeasible tasks may get in conflict with other task. If both tasks are defined by a single planner, he can define a preference between conflicting tasks during planning phase, Otherwise, during execution, delibe- ration module is used to establish preference between conflicting tasks.

4.3   Inter-leaving Planning, Execution and Deliberation

Various approaches in the literature [32, 33], including our previous work [12], have developed argumentation-based algorithms for closed-loop systems, but no work has been done to identify and model the interaction steps of argumentation when various stakeholders are involved in the risk management of an open-loop system such as logistics and supply chain that needs interleaving planning and execution. The pro- posed framework address this drawback by interleaving planning and execution.

The collaborative planning algorithm interleaving execution, integrated with argumentation-driven dialogue system works as follows:

1. Terminate the collaborative planning activity if the objective statement is satisfied in current planning phase. Return a list of tasks (situations) indicating which have been executed.
2. Check if there is an executable plan task i.e., a step which has been planned but not yet executed. if there is none, go to step 4
3. For every executable plan task, executed the task

   – Incorporate new found information from execution into planning stage.
   – if conflict arise, initiate call to deliberation module for establishment of preference over conflicting situations.
   – Go to step 2

4. Plan:

   – Either
   – – identify a objective that needs to be achieved.
   – – Add a new tasks to the existing plan step to achieve the objective.
   – Or
   – – Apply (simulate execution of) tasks previously selected to be in the plan.
   – Go to step 1

5   Conclusion

In this paper, we propose a collaborative planning and execution framework. MAP based approaches discussed in literature takes planning and execution as separate steps and as a result, most of their implementations lack real-world applications. Our work is first of its kind that provides a collaborating environment to human planners where planning interleave with the execution along with deliberation support in an open loop system like logistics and supply chain. We plan to develop a prototype system and extend the system's functionality with conflict blocking and conflict propagation based reasoning models.

References

1. Belesiotis, A., Rovatsos, M., Rahwan, I.: A generative dialogue system for arguing about plans in situation calculus. In: McBurney, P., Rahwan, I., Parsons, S., Maudet, N. (eds.) ArgMAS 2009. LNCS, vol. 6057, pp. 23–41. Springer, Heidelberg (2010)
2. Borrajo, D.: Multi-agent planning by plan reuse. In: Proceedings of the 2013 International Conference on Autonomous Agents and Multi-agent Systems, pp. 1141–1142. International Foundation for Autonomous Agents and Multiagent Systems (2013)
3. Crosby, M., Rovatsos, M., Petrick, R.P.: Automated agent decomposition for classical planning. In: ICAPS (2013)

4. Durfee, E.H.: Distributed problem solving and planning. In: Luck, M., Mařík, V., Štěpánková, O., Trappl, R. (eds.) ACAI 2001 and EASSS 2001. LNCS (LNAI), vol. 2086, pp. 118–149. Springer, Heidelberg (2001)

5. Durfee, E.H., Lesser, V.R.: Partial global planning: A coordination framework for distributed hypothesis formation. IEEE Transactions on Systems, Man and Cybernetics 21(5), 1167–1183 (1991)

6. Gabaldon, A., Langley, P.: Dialogue understanding in a logic of action and belief (2015)

7. Ghallab, M., Nau, D., Traverso, P.: The actors view of automated planning and acting: A position paper. Artificial Intelligence 208(0), 1–17 (2014). http://www.sciencedirect.com/science/article/pii/S0004370213001173

8. Janjua, N.K.: A Defeasible Logic Programming-Based Framework to Support Argumentation in Semantic Web Applications. Springer Theses, Springer International Publishing (2014)

9. Janjua, N.K.: Process map discovery from business policies: a knowledge representation approach with argumentative reasoning (kr@ pmd). In: A Defeasible Logic Programming-Based Framework to Support Argumentation in Semantic Web Applications, pp. 201–233. Springer (2014)

10. Janjua, N.K., Hussain, F.K.: Web@ IDSS–argumentation-enabled web-based IDSS for reasoning over incomplete and conflicting information. Knowledge-Based Systems 32, 9–27 (2012)

11. Kilger, C., Reuter, B., Stadtler, H.: Collaborative planning. In: Supply Chain Management and Advanced Planning, pp. 257–277. Springer (2015)

12. Kok, E.M., Meyer, John-Jules Ch., Prakken, H., Vreeswijk, G.A.: A formal argumentation framework for deliberation dialogues. In: McBurney, P., Rahwan, I., Parsons, S. (eds.) ArgMAS 2010. LNCS, vol. 6614, pp. 31–48. Springer, Heidelberg (2011)

13. McCarthy, J.: Situations, actions, and causal laws. Tech. rep., DTIC Document (1963)

14. Mott, D., Harwood, W.: Representing logic and rationale in semantic web technologies. In: The Fourth Annual Conference of the International Technology Alliance, pp. 13–17. London, England (2010)

15. Nissim, R., Brafman, R.I.: Multi-agent a* for parallel and distributed systems. In: Proceedings of the 11th International Conference on Autonomous Agents and Multiagent Systems, vol. 3, pp. 1265–1266. Richland, SC (2012)

16. Patel, J., Dorneich, M., Mott, D., Bahrami, A., Giammanco, C.: Improving coalition planning by making plans alive. IEEE Intelligent Systems 28(1), 17–25 (2013)

17. Reiter, R.: On knowledge-based programming with sensing in the situation calculus. ACM Trans. Comput. Logic 2(4), 433–457 (2001). http://doi.acm.org/10.1145/383779.383780

18. Stone, P., Veloso, M.: User-guided interleaving of planning and execution. In: Proceedings of the European Workshop on Planning, vol. 12 (1995)

19. Torreño, A., Onaindia, E., Sapena, Ó.: An approach to multi-agent planning with incomplete information. In: ECAI, pp. 762–767 (2012)

Author Index

Printed in the United States
By Bookmasters